How To Get A Good Night's Sleep

Johann Callaghan

(ITEC, IFPA, MIFPA, MWIBN)

Printed in Ireland
First print Aug 2017

Published by: JML Publications
www.johanncallaghan.com

Editorial and publishing services by

Adrian Rush MISTC, Managing Partner

AMR Enterprises

Any advice or teachings given in this book are not intended to replace the services of your physician. Nor is the book meant to provide an alternative to professional medical treatment. This book offers no medical diagnosis of or treatment for any specific medical or psychological issue you may have. Neither the publisher nor the author is engaged in rendering professional advice or services to the individual reader. All matters regarding your health require medical supervision. Neither the author nor the publisher shall be liable or responsible for any loss or damage allegedly arising from any information or suggestion in this book.

ISBN 978-1-9998014-0-3 (paperback)
ISBN 978-1-9998014-1-0 (ebook)
ISBN 978-1-9998014-2-7 (audio book)

A CIP record for this title is available from the British Library.

Typeset and Printed by

Ross Print Services, Greystones

About the Author

Johann Callaghan (ITEC, IFPA, MIFPA, MWIBN) was born in Dublin, Ireland. She is an Author, Speaker, Educator, Holistic Therapist, Clinical Aromatherapist, Entrepreneur, busy mum, Organiser of the Empowering Mind Body & Soul Expo, June 2017 and winner of Micro Biz Awards (MBA), Whatswhat.ie member of the year 2016.

After losing her baby daughter, Megan, in 2007 her whole life changed. As part of her healing, she found a new holistic way of being. After studying and practicing massage, reflexology, reiki and other holistic therapies from 2008, she decided to set up her own business 'Therapeutic Healing' in March 2013. A few years after her baby Leah arrived in 2010, Johann set up her Health & Wellness online training school http://courses.johanncallaghan.com as a form of passive income so she could spend more time with her daughter. In addition to her Health & Wellness online training school, she takes part in speaking events, her biggest one yet was the Empowering Mind Body & Soul Expo, June 2017 where she shared the stage with Health & Nutrition Specialist, Dr. Gloriane Giovannelli (Dr. Glo) and international speaker and mentor, Pat Slattery.

Johann Callaghan is passionate about empowering you to discover how you can take back control of your family's life with awareness and healthy living. Johann will help to educate and inspire you to self help your family to get on the path of happiness and wellness that you can do yourself.

Acknowledgements

My heartfelt thanks to my mum for her lifetime support and who always believed in me no matter what. My thanks to Kevin Connelly, for always encouraging me, and genuinely wanting me to succeed in life.

My thanks to Adrian Rush, my editor, who guided and directed me for a superb finish to this book and to Ross Print Services whose endless support and reassurance was very much appreciated. Also, my sincere gratitude to Brendan Sands for his time, abundant knowledge and tips. My sincere thanks to Breeda Hurley who recently published her book and gave me endless support and direction when I needed it most. My deep gratitude to all my friendly customers and clients and especially Teresa Corcoran.

I would like to acknowledge and thank Antoinette-Coleman Kelly for her support and knowledge; Barbara Gordon of Whatswhat.ie for her assistant over the years and friendship; the Women In Business Network (WIBN), Kildare for their connections and support; the We Can and We Will Group and Amanda Delaney for their fantastic energy; the Athy Toastmasters group who gave me great inspiration and courage for public speaking; CharityRadio.ie for helping to make me visible, Pat Slattery, entrepreneur and business mentor, for his relentless help in building my self belief and self worth, encouraging me to keep showing up, stepping up, setting bigger goals for bigger possibilities, being the very best I can be and setting those dates; Donna Kennedy, outstanding inspirational speaker and best selling author who strived to help me put the content of this book together; Dr. Gloriane Giovannelli for sharing the stage with me at my Empowering Mind Body & Soul Expo event and helping to make me visible; Heidi Sawyer who I owe a huge heartfelt thanks for her help. I am very grateful.

Thank you to Lauren Mc Donagh Newell, my niece, for the illustrations she created for this book.

In memory of my daughter,
Megan Newell,
for her lifetime gift to me.

CONTENTS

Figures

Tables

Introduction

As you might already know, good quality sleep is one of the most important ingredients to living a healthy, happy and successful life free of worry.

We are all living busy lives. As people can be co-dependent in relationships, we are now also becoming co-dependent with work and we lose focus on our lives. We feel that we need to work and we have no choice about that. All our time goes into getting as much done as we can, that we often overlook one of the most crucial elements of life, **sleep.**

Too often we push ourselves beyond the achievable and we are constantly sabotaging ourselves, telling ourselves stories that we haven't done enough. We don't even know what our values are and what is important to us, things that make us happy. Becoming conscious of the value of being happy and successful, whatever that is for you, involves slowing down and caring for ourselves. By making ourselves feel important and doing the best we can in life, can help us to slow down.

While we are busy keeping ourselves busy, we forget to slow down and try to use the time we have to get things done. We bring all these thoughts and emotions to bed with us trying to figure them out and keeping the brain awake. Then you have the problem of feeling stressed, weak and exhausted. The problem is that you struggle to get to sleep or to go back to sleep. The brain is always looking for what's wrong. It's a survival mechanism. It's what keeps us safe.

Quite often there is a perception that sleep is not important. If something is not important to us, then we don't value it or respect it. Sleep needs to be appreciated and acknowledged that it is vital for our overall health and well-being. We sleep for a third of our lives, so if we spend so much time sleeping, it has to be significant.

Sleep is not a waste of time. In fact, when we are asleep our bodies and our brains are very busy.

In this book, we are going to change the way you think about sleep, understand sleep and give it new healthy habits to enable good quality sleep.

For many of us, we are so desperate to sleep so we try to control it and life gets pushed aside. We can't control sleep. However, many of us try to do this with the struggle of getting to sleep. We choose not to sleep with our snoring partner, or not having children for the fear of being too tired to look after them. We are afraid that we will not be productive at work so we ring in sick. The list goes on and before we know where we are, life is put on hold. This book is for anyone for whom getting a good night's sleep has become a struggle. By facing our fears and by being vulnerable, we are coming out of our comfort zone and opening ourselves to opportunities for change. This takes courage and a change in perspectives. Think of vulnerability as an option for change. If we keep ourselves safe and try to control our environment, we will never be open to change.

Taking the first step of understanding your sleep problem will energise you into making improvements on your sleep. This will be a gentle process that will allow the natural process of sleep without the struggle.

Having confidence can contribute to how we feel, reducing anxiety and stress. Happiness comes from us not the brain. The fastest why to change our state is not in the mind, it's in your body. You can change the biochemistry of your body with power poises. Higher levels of testosterone (in both men and women) lead to increased feelings of confidence while cortisol levels reduce, leading to reduced stress.

If you sit trying to think your way out of a feeling, you will be unsuccessful. Limiting beliefs that you don't explore is the same as just accepting and resigning to them. Two things stop you from moving forward:

1. How you are feeling is what stops you physically.

2. What the belief system is that's keeping you there in the first place.

You become insightful when you are grateful and passionate. You can see beyond the blocks instead of getting tangled in negative thoughts.

Most of us think that our thoughts are our thoughts. We are unconsciously influenced by things in our environment and our thoughts develop from that. When we come back to gratitude we calm the mind. You can't be angry and grateful at the same time.

It won't work long term if you are beating yourself up to get to sleep. You need to rewire your brain to make it easier. It works differently for everyone and you have to find out your vulnerabilities. As humans, we are very addictive in nature. It is much easier having habits that we do automatically than having will power and energy to do what we should be doing.

All we have to do to maintain our health and balance is to listen to our body. We are wired to understand the language of our body and to know if we are losing our power and control of our health. How does your body talk to you? Understand choice and consequence. This is a skill you can develop and will empower you to understand and respect sleep on a deeper level giving you real results.

CHAPTER 1

The Importance of Sleep

The ability to rest is the body's key to healing. If you can't heal, you will get sick and different systems of the body begin to become affected. When you sleep, you are resting and resetting the body. Sleeping is how we reset all of our systems within the body. It's like 're-booting a computer'. You have to reset the body and shut down old programs running in the background, taking up excess energy. If you don't, it will become exhausted.

Thomas Edison hated sleep. He thought sleep was a waste of time and did as little of it as possible. Others, like Winston Churchill, loved to sleep. He credits his success in leading Britain through World War II to the naps he took. In fact, he used to keep a bed in the House of Parliament where he took regular naps.[1] Margaret Thatcher said 'Sleep is for whimps'.

If we didn't have proper sleep, we would feel moody, irritable, and foggy and lack in concentration and focus. Our whole cognitive function, how we perceive things and our reasoning, would be impaired. Our thinking, learning, judgement, decision making, planning are all affected. Our ability to adjust quickly to situations is impaired. Lack of sleep can result in our memories and experiences of the day not being consolidated into our long term memory. Our daily tasks and working memory become affected and we have difficulty doing the simplest tasks. Long term, our memory, language and speech can be affected.

Sleep loss can contribute to sleeping disorders like Sleep Apnoea and they are linked to stress and high blood pressure. Chronic sleep loss can put you at risk for heart disease, diabetes and stroke. Weight gain is another contributing factor to sleep loss because chemicals and hormones that play a key role in controlling appetite and weight gain are released during sleep.

Sleep deprivation not only has a major impact on cognitive functioning and intelligence, but also on emotional and physical health.

We are living in a very busy and fast paced society, always on the go. Most people will say they don't have time to rest especially if you are a mother or father. You have a nagging child pulling out of you, and a million and one things to do around the house, let alone organising the dinner and bedtime. Just think, if you can just take time out for a few minutes to rest, you will reap the benefits. Some people consider resting as being lazy and others that it's not possible with all the tasks at hand especially if you are a parent. If you keep going and going you will become physically and emotionally exhausted. Lack of rest or sleep will impact greatly on relationships, health, your happiness and well-being, performance and decision making. Sleep and rest keep the body and mind fit and strong. Pushing your body will result physically in tight neck, back and shoulders. Your digestion becomes a problem with all the tension in your body. This creates issues like reflux and heartburn or food not being digested properly because your body is not relaxed enough for the smooth muscle movements required to push through and digest your food. This weakens your immune system and affects your ability to regulate weight. Your hormones will start to become unbalanced from the stress hormones cortisol and adrenaline. This pushes your body into a 'fight or flight' state with the body constantly being in an alert state with all your daily demands. These fluctuating hormones cause all sorts of problems from sugar imbalance and insulin resistance to depression and chronic fatigue. This all affects your mood as you continue to focus on all that's happening to you. Your thoughts create your emotions and so you are feeling pretty low and that has an impact on your mental state. You get tired just thinking about it.

Our society is dangerously too focused on constant 'doing' and 'achieving' without any awareness of 'nourishing' and 'recharging' our bodies and minds. This awareness is of utmost importance to catch on to, before we burnout and become a society of unfriendly, unsociable, uncooperative and unproductive people. We are just too hard on ourselves and we are not great at giving ourselves credit for doing the best that we can. Be kind to yourself and have a rest. Take a break and re-charge your batteries. It is absolutely essential to do this. It can start with taking just a moment to sit down and build on it from there. You owe it to yourself. Respect yourself. Do you love yourself enough to just take some time out and have a moment of peace and feel you deserve it?

When we rest, and get away from all the mundane activities of life, we become centred and we listen to our inward world or inner self. This is the only time we can hear the conversation of our bodies when we are still. This is where we get all our insights and wisdom from. This really is a wonderful gift and we have the power to do this. **So take back your power. It's there for the taking.** All we have to do is become aware of when we feel tired and have a break.

Summary

- Not getting at least 8 hours of uninterrupted sleep per night (at night) can be just as bad as eating poorly and not exercising.
- The importance of sleep is often overlooked and is one of the most important factors to our health.
- Lack of sleep can aggravate medical problems and interfere with the body's natural ability to heal itself.
- We need sleep for muscle repair, memory consolidation, release of hormones regulating growth and appetite and a healthy immune system.

- Sleep balances our appetites by helping to regulate levels of the hormones ghrelin and leptin, which play a role in our feelings of hunger and fullness. Leptin suppresses appetite and ghrelin increases it. So when we're sleep deprived, we may feel the need to eat more, which can lead to weight gain. Even if you get plenty of nutrition, if you don't get adequate sleep you will be inclined to eat more.
- Lack of sleep can increase cortisol which increases sugar into the bloodstream, contributing to weight gain.
- Lack of sleep can inhibit the Human Growth Hormone (HGH) which is responsible for growth and repair especially in young children and teens. It is also necessary as we grow older because it increases our muscle mass, thickens our skin and strengthen our bones.
- Sleep is critical for brain detoxification

The Process of Sleep

It is thought by some that sleep is a passive process. However, it is far from passive and is actually quite an active process. A lot of processes happen in the body at night including healing and repairing that is vital to our health and well-being. Our brains are more active at night than any time during the day.

When we enter into sleep there is a process that it follows until the wakefulness. The circadian rhythm and the sleep/wake drive work together to regulate our sleep and wakefulness. Our sleep hormone, melatonin is at its peak, helping to promote sleep. Our body temperature, blood pressure and cortisol levels reduce, preparing the body for sleep and promoting the release of hormones responsible for healing and repairing the body while we sleep. As we enter into sleep we go through a number of sleep cycles throughout the night. Each cycle is typically 90 minutes. It comprises of 4 stages of Non-Rapid Eye Movement (NREM) and then Rapid Eye Movement (REM) sleep. The brain waves slow down and increase in amplitude at each stage. When we are in the REM stage, we dream. This is the only time our bodies are completely paralysed to prevent us from physically acting out our dreams. As we near the morning, our body temperature, blood pressure and cortisol levels start to rise again, preparing us for wakefulness where the cycle starts over once again.

Our autonomic nervous system activity causes changes in blood pressure and heart rate during sleep. When we wake in the morning, our blood pressure and heart rate go up quickly making it the most prone time for heart attacks. That together with stiffer blood vessels and sticky blood when we wake can also be a contributing factor for heart attacks.

Sleep Deprivation

Sleep deprivation is suffering from lack of sleep. When someone is chronically sleep deprived, also known as having a 'sleep debt', they will experience excessive daytime sleepiness and loss of focus, affecting the brain and cognitive function. When sleep deprived, micro sleeps are difficult to avoid. Micro sleeps are experienced when an individual losses awareness and has an episode of sleep which may last for only a few seconds. It is enough to cause a fatal car accident when driving a car. When a person experiences a micro sleep, they usually aren't even aware it occurred.

When you don't sleep well, you wake up feeling moody, very sensitive emotionally, cranky and foggy. Our cognitive function is impaired which makes thinking, decision making, planning and learning very difficult. Our ability to think clearly affects our memories. Sleep is critical for forming new memories and integrating them with what we know already, helping to create connections between them. Lack of sleep also makes it difficult and dangerous to operate machinery or driving a car because our reaction times are lessened. Driver fatigue is being highlighted as a contributory factor of 1 in 5 driver deaths as a result of fatal motor accidents.[2] **Driver fatigue is just as bad as drink driving. Ireland is among the highest alcohol consuming countries in the EU according to research published on November 1st 2007 by the Health Research Board.**[3] In 1 in 4 fatal crashes, the driver had consumed alcohol.[4] For driver fatigue, the RSA recommends to stop, take a cup of coffee and a 15 minute nap. *See Figure 1 Drivers Fatigue.*

Figure 1 Drivers Fatigue

This is only a small effect that sleep deprivation has on us. Over a long time, it can lead to lots of health issues both physical and mental.

So how do we know if we are sleep deprived? Many of us are not even aware that we are not getting enough sleep. Besides the obvious culprits of dark baggy eyes, it is often not acknowledged or even noticed. Here is a test from Michael Mosley, who uses a technique called the 'Sleep On-set Latency' test to see if you suffer from severe sleep deprivation.

Go to bed in the middle of the afternoon and see how fast it takes you to fall asleep.

- If you fall asleep after 15 minutes then you are ok
- If you fall asleep in 10 minutes then you are sleep deprived
- If you fall asleep in 5 minutes or less you may be severely sleep deprived.

You can determine when you wake up by holding a spoon in your hand with your thumb and index finger. When you fall asleep, it will drop out of your hand and fall on the floor waking you up (make sure the floor is hard or put something on the floor that will make a noise when the spoon falls).

Sleep is critical for your health in a multitude of ways and on many different levels. Sleep deprivation has the same effect on your immune system as physical stress or illness. Detoxification is a vital role of the immune system and allows all the waste in the body to be eliminated. The brain also needs to get rid of waste by detoxifying. The liver is the largest organ in the body (after the skin) with over 200 different jobs. Some of the most important ones are filtering and eliminating toxic substances like alcohol, chemicals, drugs, dead blood cells, metabolic waste and harmful micro-organisms. Detoxification is done primarily when we are at rest or sleeping. It is important that the liver is working optimally so that these substances are eliminated from the circulatory system and do not go deeper into the body causing diseases and ill-health. Lack of sleep can raise your risk of heart disease, diabetes, mental health problems and infertility.

In a car, you would need to have the oil filter replaced regularly to stop the build-up of dirt in the oil in order to have a smooth running car. Equally, we need to keep our circulatory system clean for a smooth functioning body.

We cannot survive without sleep. In a study, a group of 10 rats were subjected to total sleep deprivation and died or were sacrificed as a result.[5]

Quality v Quantity

The amount of sleep we get is not nearly as important as the quality of sleep we get. We experience good quality sleep when we can fall asleep within 20 minutes only wake up once during the night and easily fall back asleep, and if we are asleep for 85% of the time we are in bed. Good quality sleep enables us to enter into a deep restful, slow wave sleep, enabling our body to heal and repair. It is a vital part of our body's restorative function and brain detoxification process.

Daytime Fatigue

How well you sleep often contributes to how you perform and feel during the day. Daytime fatigue can often be reduced and managed by daily routines and lifestyle choices. Here are a few things to consider:

- Identifying and practicing sleep hygiene tips can create good habits when preparing for bed.
- Getting into sync with sleep/wake homeostasis and your Circadian Biological Clock will help you feel much more refreshed and energised.
- Get out into daylight as soon as you can after you wake up. Spend more time outdoors and use a light box during winter months when there is less daylight.

- At night time avoid bright screens from laptops, ipads, tablets and phones. The blue light interferes with the production of melatonin, the sleep hormone.
- Don't do vigorous exercises in the late evening. Athletes often have a problem with high adrenaline levels still in their system at night time effecting getting to sleep.

Weight Gain

We are designed to naturally fast between 8pm and 8am. This is a fast break our body takes. The first meal of the day is hence called 'break' 'fast'.

We have two hormones that naturally regulate our hunger appetite, ghrelin (makes us feel hungry) and leptin (makes us feel full). Ghrelin, our hunger hormone, naturally resets this cycle after a 12 hour period. If we eat late, this can't occur. When we eat late we throw out natural rhythms off. Our body temperature and hormones are set for sleep and not digestion. When we eat late, we either didn't eat enough during the day and our body is craving for quick energy or we may eat from boredom or emotional reasons. We tend to store more calories which are stored as fat because our body is entering a restful state and not metabolising as efficiently as during the day.

When we are tired, we need more energy and therefore eat more, contributing to weight gain.

Burnout and Chronic Fatigue

Burnout and Chronic Fatigue Syndrome (CFS) appear to be similar but there are some differences.

CFS, (also known as Myalgic Encephalomyelitis or ME) can be categorised as having excessive tiredness for at least six months that doesn't improve with bed rest. While the symptoms are similar, Chronic Fatigue sufferers will also experience muscle and joint pain in addition. This may lead to a widespread chronic musculoskeletal pain known as Fibromyalgia. Research shows that CFS patients have a suppressed Hypothalamic-Pituitary-Adrenal (HPA) Axis and a low response to stress and also the waking up response cortisol normally gives us in the morning.

Burnout is a state of physical, emotional and mental exhaustion caused by excessive and ongoing stress. Burnout happens when you feel like you just can't continue to do anything physically and it's emotionally draining with no motivation. Burnout can affect everything in your life from family and friends to work and how you feel about life. It occurs as a result of working excessively, being a high achiever with high levels of emotional demand. There is a sense of detachment, hopelessness and a negative outlook on life.

Burnout is a result of ongoing long term physical and emotional stress until it eventually uses all the body's resources and dries them up. It is on ongoing demand for cortisol and eventually the adrenal glands can't make enough cortisol which the body needs for energy. Burnout can also be associated with CFS and Post Traumatic Stress Disorder (PTSD).

A study on teachers showed that a positive mindset can help to handle stress and reduce the possibility of burnout. Teachers with chronic fatigue and experiencing stress had higher levels of cortisol than those who had burnout.[6] The cortisol is causing exhaustion.

Sometimes, when we reach the stage of burnout, it is giving us an opportunity to slow down and really look at what went wrong. Finding happiness again is possible and by allowing yourself to slow down, rest, reflect and build yourself up again, you can overcome burnout. It is vitally important to reach out and find someone to talk to.

Adrenal Fatigue and Stress

Most people with Adrenal Fatigue will have some form of sleep disorder. When people are suffering with exhaustion and chronic sleep deprivation, the adrenal function must not be overlooked. You may have Adrenal Fatigue, also called Adrenal Dysfunction, if you experience any of the following:

- Feeling tired very early in the evening
- When you go to bed, you are wide awake and can't go asleep
- When you do sleep, you feel like you haven't slept
- You wake up several times during the night
- You wake up groggy and exhauste

Stress can come in the form of emotional, physical, lifestyle, diet and inflammation. Stress causes cortisol to be released into the bloodstream. This hormone keeps us awake and alert preventing us from sleeping and getting our vital deep slow wave sleep. This deep sleep is vital to help heal and repair the adrenals, but this cycle is perpetuating and worsening the adrenals and our sleep.

The levels of cortisol are part of the circadian rhythm with high levels in the morning and gradually reducing in the evening. This imbalance of excess cortisol is overworking the adrenals causing them to burn out. When we experience this prolonged stress, our organs begin to suffer because our digestive system, immune system and thyroid function are impaired. These systems only work optimally when we are in a state of relaxation known as 'rest and digest'.

Healthy Skin and Pre-Mature Ageing

When we don't get enough sleep, we usually have the tell tale signs of baggy eyes, dull skin and dark circles under our eyes. When we don't get enough sleep we usually have high cortisol levels in our system. High cortisol can cause inflammation and break down our skin collagen which is a protein that helps to keep our skin smooth and supple. This can also contribute to skin conditions like Psoriasis and Eczema.

How Sleep Affects the Wheel of Life

Poor sleep impacts all areas of our lives including our physical health and mental wellbeing, our relationships and our ability to make decisions. The wheel of life takes into account all aspects of our living and lifestyle. If one part is under functioning it will affect the rest.

Personal Growth and Learning

By becoming more aware of our surroundings and getting to know ourselves better we can understand and have a much better connection with ourselves. We can reflect on our live experiences and learn from that. We can listen to what our body actually needs. However, life is so busy now and we are living at a fast pace. We are always busy doing things and achieving things in our lives. By being aware and conscious of what is going on around us instead of habitually responding to events and circumstances, we can respond more effectively. To achieve this state we need to in a state of calm and contentment. This is not possible when we have a busy mind and excess adrenaline and cortisol running through the body, keeping us awake and alert.

Fun and Recreation

We need to have some fun in our lives to let go of everyday tensions, worries and responsibilities for just a short time. Playing with children often takes us away from our mundane responsible and busy lives. However, many people will say "I don't have the time" and we don't have the physical energy.

Friends and Family

We become moody and irritable when we don't get enough sleep. This affects our relationships with our family including spouse and children and distant relationships like parents and siblings. It makes it difficult to maintain relationships, and to engage in social activities with friends' because we are too tired.

Career and Finance

We lack concentration and focus so therefore our work will be less productive and we don't get paid especially if you are self-employed. We lose our motivation and momentum, making it harder to get back into the work and get the flow going again.

Intimate Relationship

Relationships with our partners can be affected. Our mood and energy is low and our tendency for any excitement is lessened. Sex drive is reduced and can cause a strain on the relationship.

Health

Sleep is vital for your physical health. Getting enough good quality sleep helps to protect our mental health, physical health and our quality of life. When we sleep our bodies are detoxifying. This is a huge part of the healing process. When we have ongoing sleep deprivation we may experience heart disease, high blood pressure, stroke and diabetes.

Spiritually

This is the relationship with our higher power and our beliefs. We lose our positive outlook, drive and believe in ourselves when we are exhausted. When we lose faith, we begin to sabotage ourselves making us feel not good enough. We often look to blame others. This affects our relationships.

Contribution

It is in our nature to help other people. It makes us feel good about ourselves and gives us a feeling of fulfilment. The person receiving help will be very grateful and often pays it forward, helping to create a stronger community or family. When we lack sleep, we often don't have the energy to do kind gestures and this also affects people around us.

Getting Yourself to Bed on Time

We have an inbuilt mechanism that alerts us when it is time to go to sleep called sleep/wake homeostasis or sleep drive. When we have been awake for a long period of time, the sleep/wake system tells us that we need sleep. This is our indicator to go to bed at this time. Our length of sleep is reflective of how long we have been awake. It works alongside our circadian rhythm and internal body clock and acts like a timer. When this is in balance we feel the need to sleep at night and our sleeping intensity is regulated, allowing us to have a deep and restful night sleep. It is our balance between sleep and wakefulness.

CHAPTER 2

When I Just Can't Sleep

We live in a very busy world. There is so much to do, children to take care of, cooking, cleaning, work and deadlines. We quite often are going around in a state of stress and anxiety and not even aware of it. We live on automatic pilot for the most, with routine tasks and similar reactions to situations and events. As humans, we are pre-programmed to focus on what's wrong and to find solutions to what we perceive as problems. When we can't sleep, we fight against these problems and try so hard to get to sleep.

The real solution is not to struggle with it and resist it but to become conscious and aware, understand and accept how it is. In this way, we are allowing whatever the problem is to just be there, that way we are not resisting and using up our energy. We must understand how the mind works and how sleep works in order to master it without trying to control it. We can master how we behave and respond to unwanted thoughts and emotions that may come up at night.

When we are busy during the day, we are distracting ourselves from our own emotions. In other words we are unconscious of them. At night when we are lying in bed and it's quiet, our emotions start to show. Becoming conscious of our unwanted or negative emotions, and how we are feeling during the day, will help diminish or reduce them at night.

Staying Asleep

In some cases, difficulty staying asleep may be caused by Sleep Apneoa, restless legs or chronic pain. Stress can raise our cortisol level and blood sugar which contributes to waking up at night. When we eat refined foods and sugary snacks late at night, this can cause our blood sugar to spike and fall. If this happens during the night when we are asleep, it will wake us up because the cortisol will kick in to compensate the drop of blood sugar.

Night Eating

The purpose of not eating big meals three to four hours before you go to bed, is to control blood sugar and cravings. Eating late at night can cause weight gain, indigestion and interruptions with sleep. In the long term, it can lead to Type 2 Diabetes. After dinner, for most of us, we tend to get the munchies and indulge in processed snacks and sweets. Some people eat late at night, not because they are hungry, but because they are board. Others may eat because they are upset and engage in what's called 'emotional eating' or 'comfort eating'. Eating late at night can interfere with the body's internal clock. The body stores these calories as fat when we go to bed instead of burning them as energy. The body reacts differently to food at night time because there are different hormone levels, and the body temperature is lower for sleep. When you eat late at night, the body is not able to process or metabolise the food effectively as it can during the day. We also have that uncomfortable full feeling when lying in bed, stopping us from going asleep.

Hormones, cortisol and adrenaline, which are two hormones involved in the circadian rhythm can also drive us to hunger. We naturally have peaks and dips during the day. When we start to feel tired towards the end of the day, and we still have work to do, we tend to reach for a quick fix to get a boost of energy. This will only increase your insulin and may wake you during the night with hunger. However, a small protein and fibre snack shortly before going to bed may be forgiven. It won't give you that sugar rush because it slows the absorption of food and will help to control glucose intolerance.

Protein also helps to build and repair muscle tissue while you sleep.

> ***Two studies have highlighted the potential impact of timing. In a study of 420 overweight or obese people published in 2013, those who ate their major meal after 3pm lost less weight during a 20-week weight-loss program than those who ate that main meal before 3pm - even when the amount they ate, slept and exercised was the same.***[7]

If you have difficulty getting asleep, stay away from stimulating foods like caffeine and chocolate late at night. Instead eat foods that help to promote sleep like pumpkin seeds, almonds, turkey, bananas. These sleep promoting foods contain the amino acids tryptophan and serotonin which are the precursors to melatonin, the sleep hormone.

When we have poor sleep and tiredness, it can interfere with our hunger hormones namely ghrelin and leptin. Ghrelin makes us feel hungry while leptin gives us a satisfied feeling of being full. When we don't sleep enough, our body needs more energy and so activates ghrelin. This usually causes us to reach for quick convenience foods that will temporarily satisfy our hunger and energy levels. Sometimes, when we wake up and go downstairs to grab something quick, we can soon create this behaviour and association of getting up in the middle of the night. This extra meal will soon be adding to the problem of weight gain. This behaviour will lead us to believing thoughts like "I can't go asleep unless I have something to eat" and so creates a bad relationship with sleep.

Our bodies are designed to fast at night and give the digestive system a break. Digestion uses energy and so if we are going to bed shortly after a meal, the body is using energy to digest food instead of getting good quality deep sleep. Digestion of food at night is slower and is not as effective as it is during the daytime. As a result, it means going to bed with a large amount of undigested food and acid in the stomach, and this increases the risk for acid reflux. We are designed to fast during the night with breakfast being the first meal of the day. Breakfast literally means 'breaking the fast' of the night.

Wide Awake at 3am

You wake up at 3am and you look at your clock. Then you calculate how much time you have left to sleep before you have to get up. You know you need to go back to sleep and this starts a sleep struggle. All your thoughts start to flood your head about how you will not be able to perform well, or have enough energy if you don't go to sleep. So why do you wake up at 3am in the first place.

We know that caffeine can interfere with sleep, but did you know that sugar can do the same? At night, our hormones and body temperature are set for sleep and not digesting food. When we eat late we throw our natural rhythms off. When the digestion is out of balance from eating late, nocturnal hypoglycaemia (low blood sugar that occurs during the night) can disrupt sleep. In addition, when we eat simple carbohydrates, refined foods or sugary snacks before bed, they will contribute to sugar spikes in the blood. Often the body is craving glucose and that is why we eat quick fix foods that contain sugar.

So how does this contribute to waking up in the middle of the night? Just before you wake up, your blood sugar levels drop very low. When this happens the body instinctively releases cortisol into the blood stream which in turn raises the blood sugar levels. Cortisol is our awakening hormone. If our blood sugar levels are not balanced it will cause spikes and it will wake us up. Then when we wake up, we start to have a sleep struggle, sending more cortisol into the blood stream and keeping us awake.

Ensure you are eating enough during the day so you don't feel hungry late at night. Eat more fibre and some complex carbohydrates with you evening meal. This will help you feel fuller for longer and also this slows the absorption of food, reducing the possibility of blood sugar spikes.

Waking too Early

Many of us have difficulty getting to sleep or staying asleep, but there are quite a number of us who wake up too early in the morning and just can't get back to sleep. Why is this?

When you are sleeping, your subconscious mind is on overdrive. There are no distractions and so all your unfinished business, emotions and things to do are all amplified. Your brain decides you have had enough sleep and need to get up and get going with all the things you need to do and sort out.

Another important factor is that women are more affected than men waking up early. Women experience a major transition in their later years, playing havoc with hormones. This can leave them vulnerable to psychological stress like children leaving home, death in the family or close friends, moving home, work etc.

It is thought that depression is linked to waking up too early. As we get older, our sleep becomes more fragmented and we don't get as much deep restful sleep. We try to go to bed early with the hope of getting enough sleep. When we wake too early, we start to worry that we aren't getting enough sleep. This can be a vicious cycle leading to depression if prolonged.

Consider going to bed later and that maybe you need less sleep or try a new routine for a couple of weeks. This will help to synchronise your sleep/wake cycle. Write down your thoughts or 'to do's' before going to bed to get them out of your head. *See Table 1 To do List.* Use a sleep diary to help figure out your routine and sleep patterns. If you have ongoing sleep problems, or excessive daytime fatigue, be sure to see your doctor.

Write down your thoughts or 'to do' list

Table 1 To do List

Waking up Exhausted

When you wake up feeling exhausted and like you're in a fog, there are a few reasons why this could be.

Late night Facebooking

Just checking last minute messages, emails on a blue screen is lethal for keeping the brain awake. Not only does it stop the production of melatonin, the sleep hormone, it also engages the brain, activating it even more instead of it slowing down. Once you get involved in this activity, it's hard to put it away and before you know where you are, another hour has passed by. You need to disconnect from the outside world and be in your quiet haven, your bedroom. Shut off phones, laptops or any other electrical device at least an hour before bed.

Spicy Foods

Eating spicy foods or overeating late at night can leave you with indigestion and heart burn, which will interfere with your sleep. This may be contributed to the ingredient capsaicin which can increase your body temperature.[8] Spicy foods have been linked to nightmares or very vivid dreams. It is advised not to eat at least three hours before going to bed. This will help to reduce blood sugar enabling you to have a restful sleep.

Poor Sleep Pattern

When you lack in sleep from a poor sleeping pattern, not only is it hard to concentrate, feel energised and remember things, but it can also cause more serious mental health issues. Consistency is key and a regular routine to keep the body in sync and a good rhythm.

Getting into Routine

The very basics of a good and effective sleeping routine is to go to bed at the same time every night and get up every morning at the same time, even on the weekends. I know, it sounds crazy but your body clock likes to have a routine. Your sleeping pattern is determined by knowing how long your body needs to sleep for, when to go to bed and when you are sleeping too much or too little. People with a good sleeping routine and who get enough sleep have:

- Restoration and healing
- More energy
- Brain function (Learning, memories, information processing)

How Long Should I Sleep for?

It's actually a very individual thing. Once you wake up feeling refreshed and able to function during the day, then that is enough sleep.

Age is a contributing factor to how much sleep you need. Older people tend to need less sleep while young babies may need up to 16 hours.

Take a look at how your family sleeps. The amount of sleep you need can be influenced by your family genes.

Can I Sleep too Much or too Little?

The longer you are awake, the sleepier you will feel. This is your sleep drive. So typically, a person needs to be awake for about 16 hours to create enough of a sleep drive to sleep for 8 hours sleep. If you stay in bed too long, you will not create enough sleep drive for your next night's sleep.

When Should I go to Sleep?

We are habitual creatures and so is your body clock. We have our best sleep when we go to bed and wake up at the same time every day even the weekends or when we are not working.

When you have a lie in, your circadian rhythm is thrown out of routine and it resets the body clock. This is why Sunday night is often the worse night for getting a good night's sleep. People are often late more often on a Monday morning than any other day.

Consider if you are a morning lark or a night owl. The time you go to bed is affected by your genes.

Get into a routine. Go to bed at the same time and rise at the same time every day. Even if you have a later than normal night, get up at the same time you usually would.

Bad Habits affecting Sleep

Drinking Alcohol

Drinking alcohol before bed is often a way to help someone get to sleep. However, does not help us in the long term. Some people like to have a drink before bed with the intention of helping the onset of sleep. While it can get you to sleep quicker, it does prevent you from having good quality sleep. Alcohol can relax the body more and contribute to snoring. It is also common to wake up during the night or go to the bathroom because alcohol is a diuretic. Dehydration is common which may wake you up for a drink. Adenosine, the sleep inducing chemical in the brain, is increased enabling a quicker onset of sleep but then quickly eliminated contributing to waking up in the middle of the night.[9] REM sleep is therefore dramatically reduced; leaving you feeling tired the next day with a foggy head.

Eating Late

Don't eat large or heavy meals too late before going to bed, ideally at least three hours before bedtime. Eating late, can affect your overall metabolism and put stress on your body, disrupting your sleep.

Caffeine Intake

Caffeine has been called the most popular drug in the world. All over the world people consume caffeine on a daily basis in coffee, tea, cocoa, chocolate, some soft drinks, and some drugs.

Caffeine should be limited to mornings and early-mid-afternoons otherwise it will disrupt sleep patterns. Caffeine is a stimulant and it takes a long time to metabolise in the body. It has a half life of 6 – 8 hours which means it takes half of the caffeine that amount of time to eliminate out of the system.

Caffeine's main effect is on the brain. The molecular make-up of caffeine is very similar to adenosine which is the sleep inducing chemical in the brain. Caffeine binds easily to it and therefore blocks it. This inhibits the sleep drive which would normally relax the central nervous system and makes you feel tired when it's time for bed. For most people, drinking excess caffeine can disrupt the sleep-wake cycle and circadian rhythm.

Your genetic make up may affect how caffeine is broken down by your liver and medications may also react with caffeine. Drinking sugary caffeine drinks or taking sugar every time you have a cup of tea or coffee may lead to a sugar spike and then a crash.

It is important to understand that all these factors that can affect this. Take note of these things and find out how your body responds to caffeine.

Energy Drinks

Many teens and young adults are drinking energy drinks for stimulation and energy. These drinks are loaded with caffeine and sugar. These energy bombs not only have a major impact on your sleep, but they leave you feeling wired, jittery and anxious. Many energy drinks have artificial sweeteners which have a toxic load on the liver, leading to fatty liver and disease. Alcohol, a depressant, is now being mixed with stimulants like energy drinks, which mask the symptoms of being drunk or intoxicated.[10]

Using Alarms

The brain recognises the sound of an alarm clock and knows it's a signal to get up. So the alarm clock is associated with waking up. Hitting the snooze button too many times, waking up at different times, only confuses the brain and the body. Every time we go back to sleep, we start a new sleep cycle. When you wake up repeatedly partway through a sleep cycle, you're at the mercy of something called 'sleep inertia'.[11] This will leave you feeling more tired and it will take a very long time to properly wake up even after a coffee or a morning shower.

Create your own transition for sleep. Become your own sleep scientist. Ask yourself what's been on your mind recently. Be aware of push notifications, social media that are connecting us to our daily world.

Winding Down

Don't engage in anything that is stressful leading up to going to bed. Stressful activities can lead to worry and keeping you from going asleep. The last hour before bed should be dedicated to peaceful and relaxing things.

Finding a night-time routine with consistency will help the body to unconsciously recognise that it is time to wind down and switch off.

Relaxation Techniques

When you can't get to sleep, your mind is probably racing with thoughts and your body is tense. Here are some relaxing techniques to help:

- Listen to soft gentle music
- Slow deep breathing helping to activate the vagus nerve
- Hot bath with magnesium flakes and essential oils
- Meditation
- Tai Chi or Qi Qong to restore energy flow
- Visualisation. This can trick the mind into feeling safe

Best Sleeping Habits

Keeping good sleeping habits can be the simplest way to getting good quality sleep. Good sleeping habits are often referred to as good 'sleep hygiene'.

- Wind-down at least 60 minutes before bed in which you do something relaxing, such as read a book. The purpose of winding down is to tell the brain that sleep is on the way. In order to calm your mind, do a breathing or relaxation exercise. Stress hormones, adrenaline and cortisol can impede our winding down. They keep your body in 'fight or flight' mode, making it difficult to get to sleep.
- Don't eat foods high in refined carbohydrates before bed. Focus on nuts, seeds, vegetables and proteins.
- Make sure your sleep environment is quiet and dark throughout the night. Our body is interconnected with the earth. In Traditional Chinese Medicine (TCM), the Chinese clock and circadian rhythms are biology and behavioural changes that follow 24-hour cycle, responding primarily to light and darkness.
- If you're having racing thoughts or worried about the next day, write it all out on paper.
- Do you text in bed or watch You Tube or maybe catch up on your emails? Disconnect from close-range electronic devices like laptops, phones, and tablets. Install an app called 'Flux'. This will reduce the blue light coming from you screen which inhibits your hormone production (melatonin) required for the sleep/wake cycle. This can shift your whole body clock cycle.
- Ground yourself. The body is like a battery. If you walk barefoot you are getting the negative electrons from the earth helping to ground and balance the body's electrical system which may be important for setting the biological clocks, regulating circadian rhythms and balancing cortisol levels.

- Don't stay in bed if you can't sleep. Lying in bed awake can create an unhealthy link between your sleeping environment and wakefulness. Instead, you want your bed to conjure sleepy thoughts and feelings only.
- Get a good sleeping position. Sleeping with the upper body in an inclined position can reduce acid reflux and in some cases help reduce snoring. If we find it hard to get comfortable in bed, use a pillow in between your knees (if you lie on your side) or place a pillow under the back of your knees (if you have back stiffness).

CHAPTER 3

The Science Of Sleep

In order to understand sleep, we must look at the basics of sleep regulation: the structures of the brain that control wakefulness and sleep, and the external factors that can influence both. The affects hormones have on our sleep, how our brain activity determines our sleep quality, our brain health and why we dream, are a significant part of the science of sleep.

Regulating Sleep

We have periods of sleepiness and wakefulness throughout the day. There are two body systems that are responsible for this: sleep/wake homeostasis and the Circadian Biological Clock.

Sleep/Wake Homeostasis

Sleep/wake homeostasis's is responsible for the drive to go to sleep after a prolonged period of wakefulness and the waking process after we have had enough sleep which is reflective on how long we were awake. However, the Circadian Biological Clock keeps us in check throughout the day ensuring we are getting rest during the day if required to avoid burn out.

Circadian Biological Clock

The internal body clock is set by the hypothalamus, the master clock. *See Figure 2 Hypothalamus*. Our eyes act as a light sensing organ to the daylight and the darkness of night, sending this information to the hypothalamus. These light signals cause the hypothalamus to send signals to other parts of the brain that control hormones and body temperature. They set the internal time to the external world. Not only do we have a master clock in the brain, we also have internal clocks in our organs. Also known as the Chinese Body Clock, it is divided into twelve two hour intervals. Each organ is most active during its specific time. For example, the liver is most active between 1am and 3am.

Our internal Circadian Biological Clock, help us to regulate sleepiness and wakefulness throughout the day. The circadian rhythm has rises and dips throughout the 24-hour cycle. There are two periods when we experience most sleepiness and a strong drive to sleep. These are between 2am and 4am at night and in the afternoon between 1pm and 3pm. This is when we experience our afternoon slump and is worst experienced when we are already sleep deprived.

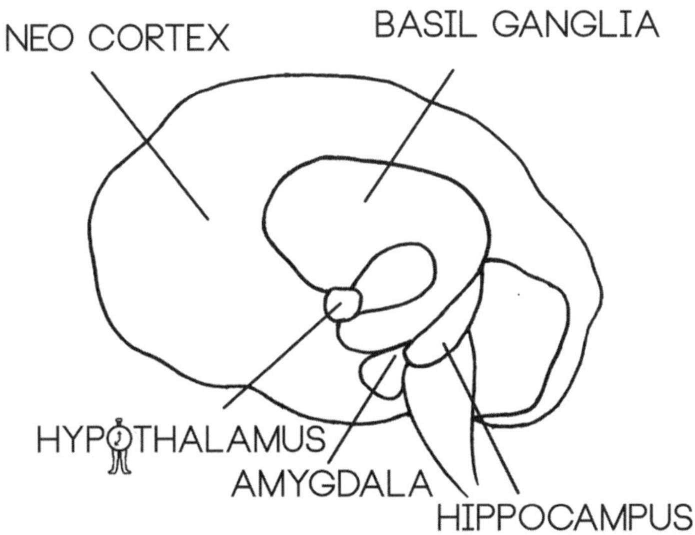

Figure 2 Hypothalamus

The Brain and Sleep

The brain has two different functional states. One is when we are awake and conscious of everything around us and the other is when we sleep.

Sleep is essential to enable the brain to maintain normal levels of cognitive skills such as speech, learning, flexible thinking and concentration. In other words, sleep plays a significant role in brain growth, repair and development. Sleep is also critical for forming our memories. Memories are reactivated during sleep by being spontaneously replayed when we are asleep. This can also help with association and solving problems by becoming more innovative and creative.

The brain also needs to get rid of waste by detoxifying. Toxins are a by-product of all the neuro-activity during the day. If we don't, this can lead to foggy brain, the inability to make decisions and reduce concentration. Long term it can also lead to neuro-degenerative diseases of the brain like Parkinson's and Alzheimer's which damage the myelin sheets of the nerve cells. *See Figure 3 Nerve Cell.*

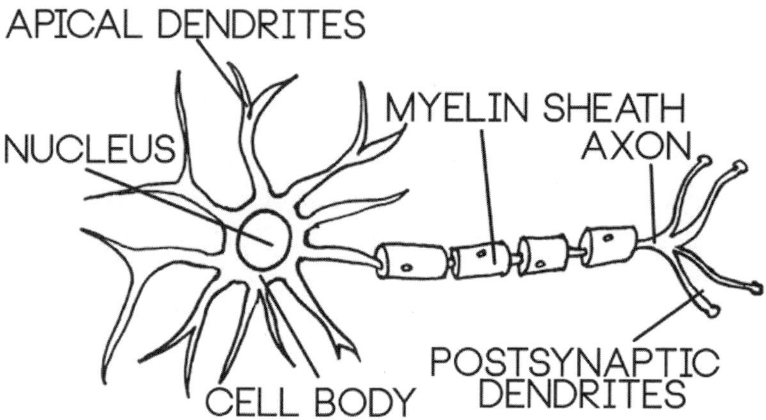

Figure 3 Nerve Cell

Detoxifying is part of the work of the glial cells, part of the glymphatic system, which is very similar to the lymphatic system in the body. It is the immunological protection to the brain. It is most active when the body is sleeping and in an unconscious state. The brain cells shrink which increases the outer space, allowing the Cerebral Spinal Fluid (CSF) to flow more in the brain and flushing out all the toxins into the body.[12] This is how toxins get into the body to be filtered by the liver. There is a toxic protein called beta-amyloid which is known to accumulate in Alzheimer's patients.[13] Sleep has been known to decrease the levels of this toxic protein and reducing the risk of brain degenerative diseases like Alzheimer's and Dementia.

A group of researchers tested this by injecting dye into the CSF. They monitored their electrical brain activity. When they were in an unconscious state their brain cells decreased and the outer brain cell space increased by 60% increasing the flow of fluid.[14]

So a good night rest can literally clear the brain!

Adenosine is a sleep promoting chemical. This builds up during wakefulness helping to induce sleep, making us feel tired, part of the sleep/wake homeostasis. [15]

Neurotransmitters are the chemical messengers of the brain that play a major role in how we function. There are two types of neurons. Excitatory neurons, like adrenaline and noradrenaline, will respond with an action. Inhibitory neurons, like serotonin and Gamma Aminobutyric Acid (GABA), will inhibit an action. One of the most abundant neurotransmitters in the human body is Acetylcholine (Ach). It is responsible for the theta wave brain state which enables the formation of memories, speech, learning and concentration.[16]

Acetylcholine is associated with muscle tone, so an adequate supply will contribute to muscles not being too relaxed and not being too tight. Proper muscle tone has been found to play a role in REM sleep and so the phrase 'sleep tight.' Acetylcholine is active in the motivation and reward centre of the brain. By stimulating the vagus nerve, which is connected to the brain, helps to release acetylcholine, which helps to reduce inflammation. Acetycholine also enables brain plasticity.

Neuroplasticity is the ability of the brain to form new neural pathways from learning or experiences. The lack of neuroplasticity could be a huge contributor to keeping us stuck in old patterns and in conditions like Attention Deficit Hyperactivity Disorder (ADHD).

Deterioration of acetylcholine in the brain has been related to the onset of Alzheimer's disease and other degenerative diseases.

Sleep Hormones

Transitions between wakefulness and sleep are controlled and regulated by the brain, which also plays a key role in directing quantity and depth of sleep. Tryptophan (amino acid) and serotonin are precursors to melatonin, the sleep hormone. Serotonin is a neurotransmitter made in the gut. This is responsible for keeping us relaxed and helping us feel good. It contributes to our moods and behaviours. Melatonin is produced in the brain by the pineal gland responsible for the sleep cycles. The growth hormone is secreted when we are in a deep sleep allowing the body to heal and repair and grow. Hormones released into the system during sleep contribute to the overall healing and restoration of the body while the brain is active in sending electrical signals for this process to occur.

Brain Waves

Beta brain waves are associated with normal waking consciousness and a heightened state of alertness, logic and critical reasoning. This is when we are alert, talking and listening.

During sleep we can access our subconscious mind and our emotions. This is a time when we clear out emotional toxins and replay the day's events in order to store them. We have five different brain frequencies (beta, alpha, theta, delta, and gamma) and most are relevant in each of the stages of sleep cycles.

NREM and REM Sleep

Sleep architecture refers to the basic structural organisation of normal sleep. There are two types of sleep, Non-Rapid Eye Movement (NREM) sleep and Rapid Eye Movement (REM) sleep. NREM has 4 different stages or cycles, each with its own or brain wave activity. REM is the deepest sleep and follows the 4 stages of sleep in NREM sleep. We spend about 70% of our sleep in NREM (Stages 1 – 4) and the remaining 30% in REM sleep.

Sleep Cycles

Some people experience a restful night of deep sleep, nothing disturbs them and they wake up feeling refreshed. Then there are those who go to bed early and sleep very lightly. They wake up feeling more tired than when they went to bed. This can be explained by the stages of sleep and sleep cycles.

When we sleep we experience a process of NREM and REM occurring continuously throughout the night approximately every 90 minutes. The first cycle is the shortest and the following cycles are longer typically 90 – 120 minutes. As a person passes into deeper stages of sleep, the brain waves slow down and become larger. During the night, these cycles of slow wave and REM sleep alternate, with the slow wave sleep becoming less deep and the REM periods more prolonged until waking occurs. *See Figure 4 Sleep Phases.*

As we sleep, our brains pass through all five stages of sleep – stages 1, 2, 3, 4 and REM sleep. This makes one complete cycle. One cycle lasts approximately 90 minutes. Most adults sleep for about 4 – 5 cycles. The order of the cycles is stage 1, 2, 3, back to stage 2 and then into REM and it continues in that order.[17] The length of each stage depends on how old you are and how long you've been asleep.

Sleep cycles and stages can be measured with the use of an Electroencephalographic (EEG) machine which records the electrical activity of the brain waves. Other instruments are used to measure muscle tone and eye movement.

When we enter into late adulthood, our slow waves become less frequent. Elderly adults experience shorter periods of slow wave sleep and less cycles during the night. Their sleep becomes very light and broken.

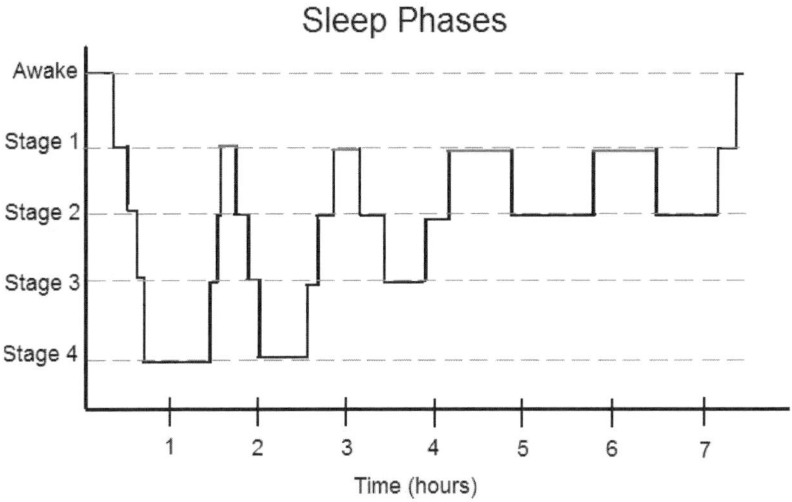

Figure 4 Sleep Phases

NREM (Stage 1)

During stages of wakeful relaxation, brain waves become slower, increase in amplitude and become more synchronous. This stage usually lasts about 7 minutes. It is a very light sleep and we can be easily awakened in this stage. People often feel awake during this stage but are actually asleep. Alpha waves are present in this stage. These brain waves are associated with daydreaming, or practicing mindfulness or meditation. Here, we can program the mind for success. It is the gateway to your subconscious mind. Alpha brain waves are 7 – 14 Hz (Cycles per second).

NREM (Stage 2)

This stage normally lasts for about 15 minutes and increases with each successive cycle during the night. In this stage, we are truly asleep. Breathing and heart rate start to slow down. Generally, noises are most likely to wake people during this light, non-REM cycle. In this stage, we can sometimes feel like we are falling, which leads to hypnic jerks (an involuntary sudden twitch which occurs just as a person is beginning to fall asleep). Sometimes it can give you a fright but it's only the muscles deeply relaxing. This stage is important for memory consolidation. This is also where we access our chakra centres, otherwise known as our energy centres. Here is a sense of deep spiritual connection. It's the mental state which you consciously create your reality. We spend most of our overall sleeping time in this stage. Theta waves are present in this stage. Theta brain waves are 4 – 7 Hz.

NREM (Stage 3)

Delta waves are the slowest (low frequency) and largest brain waves (high amplitude) and we experience this when we are in a deep sleep. You do not dream in this state and are completely unconscious. Delta brain waves are 0 – 4 Hz.

NREM (Stage 4)

This is the deepest stage of sleep called slow wave sleep. If you wake up during this stage, you will be groggy and dazed for a while. Delta is the realm of your unconscious mind, and the gateway to the universal mind and the collective unconscious. Some children experience bed wetting, night terrors or sleep walking during this stage. Deep sleep with slow wave activity is very important for preventing long term disease. This stage is linked to deep healing. Therefore, not having enough of this sleep is detrimental to your health.

REM

Rapid Eye Movement occurs after the first 4 stages of NREM sleep. This is the stage when most dreams occur. Our emotions are processed when we dream. This helps to sort out our unfinished feelings and emotions and may help prevent depression. Young children and babies typically spend about twice as much time as adults in REM sleep. Our brain activity is at its most active. Our blood pressure and breathing rises. We are completely unconscious and our body is paralysed. This prevents us from acting out our drcams. We have about 3 – 5 REM episodes a night.

Blood flow increases to the limbic area of the brain, more so than during wakefulness. This area as we know is involved in emotions, visualisations and memories.

The sympathetic nervous system activity reduces as NREM gets deeper lowering heart rate and blood pressure.

Tip: It takes the average human about 15-20 minutes to fall asleep. A good night's sleep consists of about 5 complete sleep cycles (depending on age). To wake up refreshed at 8:00 AM, you should go to bed at either 10:45 or 12:15. If you wake up at one of these times, you'll rise in between 90-minute sleep cycles. See Table 2 Sleep Stages.

Stage	**Sleep**	**Brain Waves**	**Wave Cycles**	**Wake up**
NREM (1)	Light	Alpha	7 – 14 Hz	Conscious, easily woken
NREM (2)	Truly Asleep	Theta	4 –7 Hz	Asleep, easily woken by noise
REM (3)	Deep Sleep	Delta	0 – 4 Hz	Very hard to wake
NREM (4)	Deepest Sleep	Delta	0 – 4 Hz	Very hard to wake
REM	Rapid Eye Movement	Alpha, Beta	14 – 25 Hz	Asleep, easily woken by noise

Table 2 Sleep Stages

Dreams

Dreams can provide us with meaning and self-discovery and insights about our lives and our emotions. Dreaming is an option of discovery our shadows enabling us to find our unconscious shadows. Some people dream while others don't recall dreaming much at all. There are lots of resources out there like books, videos, online information or go to a workshop. This prerequisite is recalling your dreams. Value your dreams and especially your nightmares. Lucid dreaming is used as a mind training method by Tibetan Buddhists. The shadow is our dark side and is incompatible with who we think we are and so we don't live our life to our full truth.

Have you ever woken up from a really good dream and try to fall back asleep quickly to go back into the dream? Lucid dreams or vivid dreams usually occur during REM sleep. The first REM phase occurs 90 minutes after you fall asleep. Later REM phases last longer and this is when you are more likely to have a lucid or vivid dream.

Lucid dreaming is when you know you're dreaming and can have some control over the dream including the character, the environment and the outcome. This awareness can be just a faint recognition. The dream can be so realistic that the brain thinks it is real and behaves as if it was awake. You can train yourself to become conscious of dreaming with the ability of being able to recall your dreams. If you set your alarm clock 15 minutes earlier than your normal wake up time, you will be in REM sleep and more likely to remember your dream. Practice using a dream journal or recording device to write down your dreams as soon as you wake up. *See Table 3 Dreams*.

Write Down Your Dreams

Table 3 Dreams

Listen to binaural beats. Binaural beats music is used as a form of 'brainwave entrainment' – a process used to entrain the brain into different states. This promotes a positive outlook helping with personal development and well-being. If you send a different sound frequency to each ear, your brain will interpret the two sound waves' overlapping pattern as an audio beat even though no beat is included in the sound. This definitely changes the brain's electrical activity, but so far scientists are unsure whether this can actually stimulate lucid dreaming.[18] There are many websites out there with collections of binaural beats, so it's easy to try it out if you can sleep with ear buds in. These beats mimic theta brain waves, which occur in REM sleep.

CHAPTER 4

Dealing with Sleeping Disorders

You could have a sleeping disorder if you have any kind of disturbance affecting you getting asleep at night or staying asleep resulting in feeling exhausted the next day.

70 million Americans suffer with sleeping disorders and the majority don't even realise they have one. People who are suffering with chronic sleep deprivation are not getting enough sleep voluntarily because their lifestyle is too hectic and busy. Our perception on sleep is that we don't have enough time to sleep and as a result, sleep is sacrificed.

How we perceive things, our mood and our attitude can all contribute to sleep disorders. Normal sleep is composed of getting ready to go to sleep, going into a light sleep, becoming disconnect from our surroundings, our breathing levels out and becomes deeper. Then the blood supply goes to our muscles for repair, tissues are regenerated and hormones are released for growth and repair. When we experience irregular sleep cycles or don't go through the proper sleep stages, then we often experience a sleep disorder. For example people with narcolepsy fall asleep suddenly by entering into a deep REM sleep bypassing the first stages of sleep and NREM sleep.

People with sleeping disorders, can experience memory loss, lack of focus and concentration the next day. Long term fatigue and exhaustion as a result of sleeping disorders, can cause other serious health conditions like heart disease, obesity and depression. If you suspect you have a sleep disorder, visit a primary care physician, mental health professional, or sleep disorders clinic.

A sleep study allows your doctor to measure how much and how well you sleep. It also helps show whether you have sleep problems and how severe they are.

Sleep Apneoa

Sleep Apneoa (derived from "Apnea," a Greek word meaning, "without breath") is a serious sleep disorder, in which a person has difficulty breathing during sleep. **There are approx 7,500 patients diagnosed in Ireland with Obstructive Sleep Apnoea (OSA) according to Irish Sleep Apnoea Trust (ISAT).** [19] The cause of Sleep Apneoa is when the muscles and soft tissue at the back of the throat relax. This causes the airways to narrow, making it difficult to breath. *See Figure 5 Sleep Apneoa.* The oxygen supply is dramatically reduced in the bloodstream which affects the energy production of all the cells in the body. The brain can sense this and causes you to arouse into a different position and will feel like a choking sensation or a gasp for air. This can happen several times in one hour throughout the whole night. This fragments the sleep and denies the body of deep restful sleep.

The most common type is OSA. It is often accompanied with snoring and brief periods where breathing stops. Sleep Apneoa and high blood pressure have both been linked to significantly increased risk for serious complications, such as stroke and heart attack. People who are most prone to Sleep Apneoa are men who smoke, drink alcohol, family history, have a thick neck or are obese.[19]

Another type of Sleep Apneoa is Central Sleep Apneoa (CSA), which occurs when your brain doesn't communicate correctly with the muscles that control breathing.

Complex Sleep Apneoa Syndrome (CompSAS) is when a person has both forms of Sleep Apneoa. If you think you may have any type or

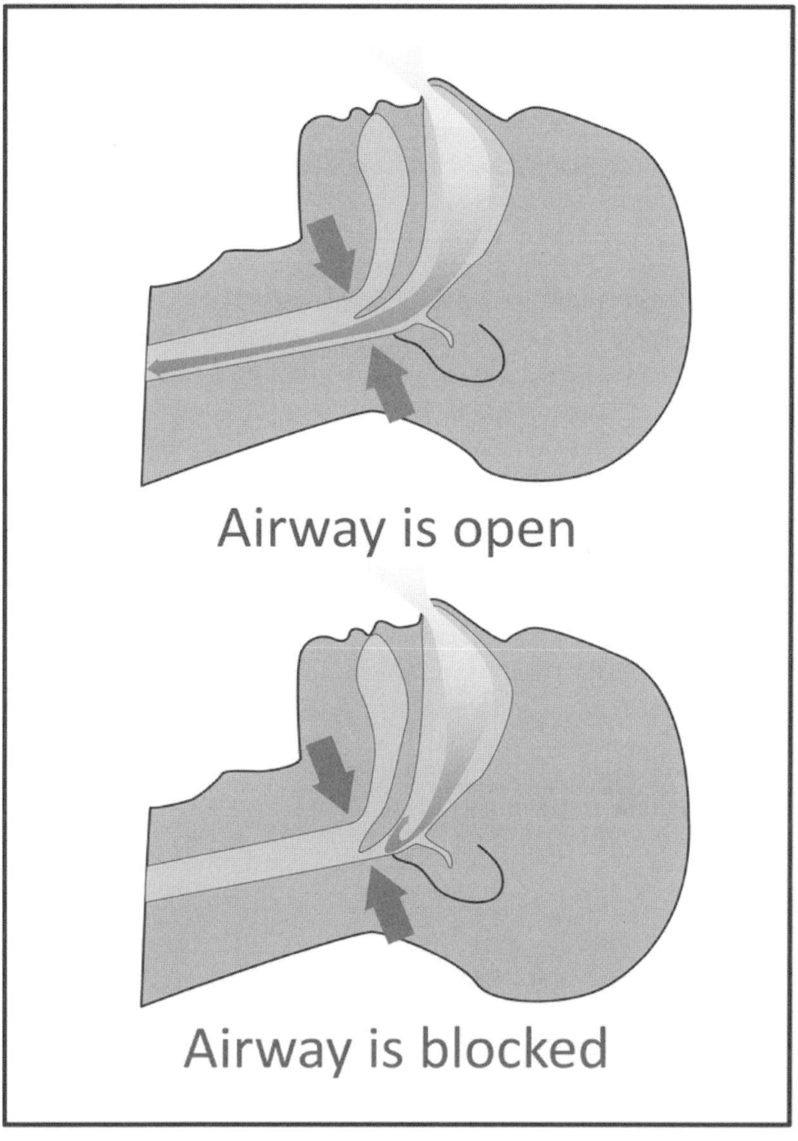

Figure 5 Sleep Apneoa

if you snore very loudly, you should see your doctor. This is a serious condition and getting treatment may help against heart disease and other health problems.

Sleep Apneoa can have serious complications like excessive tiredness during the day. It can cause high blood pressure because of the lack of oxygen in the blood which causes a strain on the heart. This in turn can lead to heart palpitations, irregular heart beat and stroke. If you are going for surgery, using medication to help with sedation is a problem when you already have breathing difficulties, so you must inform the doctor before surgery. Sleep Apneoa can affect relationships, often sleeping in separate rooms because of the sleep disturbance.

Sleep Apneoa can also have a devastating impact on our microbiome, which is responsible for a variety of bodily functions including gut and brain health and making the neurotransmitter serotonin, the precursor to melatonin. Our gut is home to trillions of microbes which have a variety of health benefits including helping to keep our hormones in balance and our neurotransmitters working optimally, nutrient formation and absorption. When blood pressure rises as a result of lack of oxygen, the bacteria can become altered. This can result in Dysbiosis – this imbalance of friendly and bad bacteria can cause inflammatory problems like Small Intestinal Bacterial Overgrowth (SIBO), which can result in Irritable Bowel Syndrome (IBS) and Ulcerative Colitis and other systemic infections.

High blood pressure, Type 2 Diabetes and obesity have been linked to men with low testosterone.

A study published in the Journal of Clinical Endocrinology and Metabolism in 2002 suggests that many men with Sleep Apneoa also have low testosterone levels.[20]

Testosterone is required for the cells to absorb blood sugar with insulin. Men with low testosterone often have insulin resistance which leads to diabetes and obesity.

A dentist or orthodontist can fit you with a mouthpiece if you have mild Sleep Apneoa. It is custom made and will help to position the jaw to allow the airways to stay open. Continuous Positive

Airway Pressure (CPAP) is sometimes used to help keep the airways open by gently blowing air into the airways. Some people find it uncomfortable to wear at night, but it may just be a case of getting used to it. It's the most common treatment for adults with moderate to severe OSA.

Avoid smoking and try to lose some weight and exercise regularly. Eat anti-inflammatory foods like turmeric, ginger, green vegetables, omega 3 and berries. Sleep on your side rather than on your back. Avoid alcohol, use sprays for your nose or nasal decongestants to keep the nasal passages open.

Snoring

Many of us are affected by snoring, whether it is you who snores or your partner. It can be very annoying, irritating and it interferes with sleep. Many people who snore are often quite irritable and tired. During sleep, the muscles in the throat and the mouth relax. The windpipe, which carries air into the lungs, narrows as a result and impedes the flow of air. When air comes into the narrow airways, the relaxed soft tissues at the back of the throat vibrate, which is what the snoring noise is. Snoring affects many people and the majority of loud snorers may have Sleep Apneoa. When you sleep next to someone who snores, you lose approximately 1 hour of sleep per night. If the snoring is loud, it will lead to sleeping in different bedrooms and causing problems in relationships and marriages. People with short wide necks are most prone to snoring because the muscles around their windpipe can't support the fat in the neck when the person is asleep. As a general rule, anyone with a collar size of 16.5 inches or more is likely to snore. Some sleeping tips for snorers are:

- Avoid alcohol. It only relaxes the muscles in the neck/throat even more.
- Lie on your side. When you sleep on your back the tongue falls back into the throat, making you more likely to snore.
- Lose some weight. The extra weight around the neck puts pressure on the windpipe when you sleep.

- Use an oil diffuser in the room at night. This humidifies the air helping to moisten the airways.
- Use nasal decongestants, nasal strips to keep nasal airways open.
- Make sure you are going to bed early and getting enough sleep.
- nhaling hot steam and essential oils may help open up the airways and reduce inflammation from possible allergies.
- A saline nasal spray can also help reduce mucus or any possible infections.

If you have tried everything and still can't get to the bottom of snoring, you may be experiencing OSA. Use a sleep tracking app like 'Sleep Time' to find out about your sleeping pattern during the night. This can tell you a lot about the quality of your sleep and if your sleep is very fragmented and broken. You can use this on flight mode, so you don't need to worry about Wi-Fi signals while you sleep. If you do suspect any form of Sleep Apnea, visit your doctor.

Insomnia

Insomnia is when someone can't get asleep, stay asleep at night or wakes up too early in the morning. People with insomnia often experience fatigue, low energy, difficulty concentrating and focusing, irritability, mood disturbances, and decreased performance in work or at school. Chronic insomnia is disrupted sleep that occurs at least three nights per week and lasts at least three months. Insomnia may be caused by a combination of things like a medical issue, psychological problems, medications or other sleeping disorders. Maintaining a healthy lifestyle along with cognitive behaviour therapy and changing the way you think about sleep are very effective ways to help overcome insomnia.

Narcolepsy

Most of the time people with narcolepsy have occasional fits of falling asleep. It is a neurological disorder. People with this condition go straight into REM sleep and it usually lasts for about five minutes. People with narcolepsy are thought to have low levels of the excitatory neurotransmitter histamine, which wakes us up.[21] Other neurotransmitters responsible for keeping us awake are dopamine and noradrenaline.

A study showed that people with narcolepsy have increased amounts of neurons that produce histamine (a wake promoting neurotransmitter). It is known by researchers that narcolepsy is caused by the loss of orexin (also called hypocretin) neuropeptides. The increase in histamine may be a compensatory response to the loss of orexin neurons.[22]

Restless Leg Syndrome

Restless Leg Syndrome (RLS) is a sensitising condition of the nervous system causing a tingling or painful feeling in the legs. It often happens towards the end of the evening or when lying down. These symptoms cause an irresistible urge to move the legs causing difficulty going or staying asleep. It can severely interfere with sleep causing extreme tiredness the next day and have an impact on the quality of life.

It is not known exactly what causes RLS however there are a few associations to it:

- **Chronic diseases** – There are some diseases and medical conditions that can have symptoms of RLS including iron deficiency, kidney diseases and diabetes.
- **Medications** – Some medications containing anti-histamines can irritate and trigger RLS.[23]
- **Pregnancy** – Some women may experience these symptoms during the last three months of the pregnancy.

I personally experienced this excruciating and debilitating nervous symptom disorder, resulting in not only extreme tiredness but also very low depressing mood. I would have given anything to sleep. It was torture.

Your doctor may carry out a blood test to determine if you have enough red blood cells or if you have enough haemoglobin, a protein in the red blood cells that contains oxygen. Ferritin may also be measured in someone with RLS.[24] A Ferritin test determines how much iron is stored in the body. Iron is required to transport oxygen in the blood and also in the tissues. If iron is deficient, it can result in anaemia. These tests can determine the level of iron stores (ferritin) and blood iron levels in the body. Ferritin is stored inside cells whereas iron is released in the blood and tissues. It is possible to have a lot of ferritin stored in the body while low blood iron levels. This indicates that there is a problem with the ferritin protein releasing iron into the blood.

Women more commonly experience it and most people affected are middle-aged or older. It is advised to avoid stimulants like caffeine and smoking as much as possible especially in the evening.

Natural Treatments for RLS

Here are some natural treatments to try for Restless Leg Syndrome:

- Gentle leg massages
- Hot baths with magnesium flakes
- Do some moderate movement and stretch the legs
- Use ice or heat packs
- Take regular walks
- Keep hydrated and drink plenty of water
- Quinine in tonic water is thought to help leg cramps and RLS.[25] *(It helped to ease my restless legs)*
- Drink a glass of water with a quarter teaspoon of good quality Himalayan salt
- Use a magnesium spray. Magnesium is our natural tranquiliser and muscle relaxant

CHAPTER 5

Sleeping Aids

You may have tried everything to help you sleep like exercise, reducing caffeine, switching off devices and adhering to sleep hygiene practices, and still you are having no success. This constant struggle can leave you feeling helpless and desperate to do anything to get asleep and feel rested for the next day.

Some people who are having regular problems with sleep may actually have an underlying health disorder like a thyroid problem or a sleep disorder. So it is important to see your doctor if you have these ongoing problems with sleep.

Some people may turn to over the counter medications to help with sleep or visit their doctor to find some solutions and/or prescribed medications. There is a stigma with prescription medication for helping to get asleep, so while this may not be the desired solution for some, it may be necessary to get some much needed rest.

Before you choose to use sleep aids, check out this list:

- If you are currently on medications, check with your doctor before using over-the-counter sleep aids as they may interfere with other medications.
- Over-the-counter sleep aids are usually designed for short term use.
- Don't drink alcohol with any medications.

- Herbal remedies and natural supplements may interfere with medications. Always seek advice from your health care practitioner or doctor.

Sometimes, a co-dependency relationship can be developed with sleeping aids. There can be a psychological problem attached to sleeping aids, believing that we can't sleep without them.

Medications must be taken properly otherwise you may not have the desired results. 50% of people use sleep aids incorrectly. You need at least 8 hours of sleep when you take medication to aid sleep or you will feel groggy when you wake up. Taking some medications and sleeping for 5-6 hours will result in you feeling worse, disorientated and foggy. If you stop taking these medications suddenly after using for a short term, you may get rebound effects. This leads you to think that you need to keep taking these medications which couldn't be further from the truth.

When medications are taken over a few nights, the brain receptors become less sensitive and therefore the effects become less effective.

The placebo effect or response is quite remarkable. This happens when a patient's symptoms improve simply because they have an expectation after taking what they think is medication when in fact it could just simply be a saline solution. They believe it will work. Over a dozen clinical studies showed that half of the benefits of taking sleeping medications benefited from the placebo effect.[26]

There can be a concern of dependency and abuse. Most doctors will advise to start off slowly and with a low dose for a short term. Also, reduce them slowly when coming off them. So they need to be used mindfully and strategically and under your doctor's instructions.

Over-the-Counter (OTC) Sleep Aids

Most over-the-counter medication is designed to work for short term. When they are used for a few nights in a row, they become less effective as the body gets used to it. Some common over-the-counter medications contain anti-histamines as the active ingredient.

These are used usually for treating allergies and colds and can cause drowsiness. They block histamine which is an alerting or wakeful neurotransmitter. Here are some anti-histamine ingredients:

- Diphenhydramine (found in brand names like Nytol, Sominex, Sleepinal, Compoz)
- Doxylamine (brand names such as Unisom, Nighttime Sleep Aid)[27]

Some other over-the-counter medications contain a combination of anti-histamines and other active ingredients to help relieve pain. While it is generally considered safe to take over-the-counter medications, it is advisable to check with your pharmacist for potential side effects or if you are taking any other medications that they may interfere with.

The main side effect with these types of medications is the drowsiness experienced the following day causing dizziness and forgetfulness. It is advised not to use them long term.

Prescribed Sleep Medication

Benzodiazepines are often referred to as a sedative and a hypnotic. They work on the central nervous system, helping to slow it down and acting as depressants. They are much stronger than over-the-counter medications and the use is controlled or prescribed by a doctor. They are used to treat sleeping problems caused by anxiety. There is a higher risk of becoming dependent on these types of medications. Sometimes, you may believe that you can't sleep without them. This in turn causes your brain to be tricked into feeling that sleeping medication is the right solution and justifies the need to take them just to sleep.

Anti-Depressants as Sleep Aids

Stress and depression can disrupt calming and feel good neurotransmitters like serotonin, dopamine, noradrenaline, and other brain chemicals. This can also interfere with moods and memory causing anxiety and worrying. Anti-depressant medications can alter brain chemicals like serotonin and noradrenaline to create a sedating effect. Anti-depressant medication is primarily used to treat depression. However, it is sometimes used in addition to help the person with sleep issues.

Waking Up Drowsy

Feeling tired or drowsy is a common side effect of most medications. This falls into certain categories of medication like narcotics (for pain), anti-depressants, anti-anxiety and anti-histamines that can cause drowsiness. It is advised to avoid driving, or anything that requires mental alertness while taking these medications.[28] Even if the medication doesn't cause drowsiness, alcohol can react with the medication causing drowsiness, so always avoid alcohol.

When taking any kind of sleeping medication, it is advised to get a full 8 hours sleep for the medication to work optimally. If not, it will leave you feeling groggy and waking up drowsy. If you are taking sleeping medication for the first time, start it when you know you don't have to be up early in the morning for an appointment. Alternatively, take your sleeping medication if you can go to bed early and get a full 8 hours in bed before you have to rise.

Natural Sleeping Supplements

Most natural products have the risk of interacting with other drugs. Always talk with your doctor if you are currently taking other medications.

Melatonin is a natural hormone produced in the body to help promote sleep. How much daylight you get affects the amount of melatonin that is made in the body. A healthy circadian cycle will keep sufficient levels of melatonin. However, in the winter time when daylight levels are low, for some of us, this can affect how much melatonin is made and contribute to Seasonal Affective Disorder (SAD) also know as 'the Winter Blues'. Melatonin supplements are sometimes used to help overcome this as well as jet lag and for people who work night shifts. It may be helpful to get back into a natural sleeping rhythm after shift work or travelling across the world. Melatonin is not very helpful if suffering from anxiety or worry. As melatonin is a hormone, it may be wise to get blood works done before opting for this option and check with your doctor.

Chamomile is one of the most ancient medicinal herbs known. Chamomile herbal tea is a long time used and popular remedy for helping to sleep well. It has relaxing and calming properties. It is also known for helping with any kind of inflammation and gastrointestinal problems.

Valerian root (Valeriana officinalis) is a sedative herb that has been used for centuries. It is typically used to help with anxiety and trouble getting to sleep. It is thought that valerian root helps to promote levels of Gamma Aminobutyric Acid (GABA) in the brain, helping to calm the body and aid sleeping. This helps the mind and body to relax, aiding in stress management and may help to lower blood pressure. Pregnant women or breast feeding and children under 3 years are advised against using it.[29] If you have other health issues, check with your doctor before taking Valerian root. It can be bought as a dry powered extract, herbal tea or tincture in most health shops.

L-tryptophan is an essential amino acid which means the body can't make it and it must be obtained in food. L-tryptophan is used to make serotonin which in turn is used to make melatonin, our sleep hormone. L-tryptophan is present in milk. Some people like a glass of warm milk to help them feel drowsy before bed.

Passion Flower is used for promoting sleep and anxiety resulting in Gastrointestinal (GI) upset.

Hop flowers are traditionally known to be used in beer. They have natural sedative and calming effects. When used together with valerian they have a powerful effect helping to combat anxiety and nervous tension, helping to relax and promote sleep.

Melissa Dream, a natural supplement in tablet form contains lemon balm, chamomile and L-theanine. These ingredients help to calm the mind and relax the body, helping to prepare for sleep. You can also diffuse melissa essential oil, also known as lemon balm oil, which may help with headaches, anxiety and hypertension.

Kevin Connolly from healthyliving.ie recommends Melissa Dream or A.Vogel Dormeasan Valerian-Hops oral drops.

Magnesium is our natural tranquiliser. 85% of people are deficient in magnesium. It is responsible for hundreds of processes in the body. We need it to relax the muscles, synthesis of protein, regulating fluid in and out of cells and enable our GABA to work optimally. The GABA neurotransmitters help our brain waves to slow down and stop the body from holding tension. If you experience muscle cramps, restless legs, going to the toilet a lot, twitchy eyes or tight muscles then you may need more magnesium. Magnesium oil spray is excellent for those tight muscles or a hot bat with magnesium flakes (magnesium chloride) will send you on your way to a good night sleep. Magnesium chloride is the compound you find in magnesium supplements. Magnesium chloride is not recommended to be ingested but it is more effective when used topically like in an oil spray or a bath. It is much more easily absorbed into the body than that of Epsom salt.

An Epsom Salt Bath also contains magnesium (magnesium sulfate) and can also help with a good night sleep. This detoxifying bath is great after exercising for sore or tight muscles. However, this type of bath may leave you feeling dizzy if you suffer with blood pressure issues. Always drink plenty of water before and after a detoxifying bath. Refrain from taking one if you are already frail or on a lot of medication.

Some cautions that should be considered when taking an Epson Salt Bath are:

- An Epson Salt Bath is a therapeutic bath and should be treated with respect.
- When having your first Epsom Salt Bath, ensure there is someone in the house.
- If you are unwell, tired or underweight start of with one-third of the suggested amount of Epsom salts.
- Do not have an Epsom Salt Bath if you suffer with high blood pressure, a serious heart condition or are pregnant.
- Get out of the bath slowly as you could be light headed.

A study was done to show this using electroencephalography (EEG) in rats.[30]

L-theanine can help to slow down brain waves. This can help to promote a deep and restful sleep.

Scientists have investigated how L-theanine can improve mood with its ability to cross the blood-brain barrier and change the amino-acid levels affecting serotonin and other mood enhancing neurotransmitters in the brain.[31]

Are Sleeping Aids Right for You?

When we are absolutely exhausted and just need some sleep, we are desperate to do anything to get a good night sleep. However, reaching for some over-the-counter sleeping medications might not be the answer for you. It could be something very simple causing this difficulty like too much caffeine or using electronic devices with the blue screen right before bed. You could be worrying excessively about what someone did to you or an upcoming event. Sleeping medications will not solve this as these problems will come up again for you. However, there is a time and a place for sleeping medications like after surgery or an extremely traumatic event.

Sleeping medications really are a temporary solution and at worst if they are used too much as a crutch, you may become dependent and even addicted to them.

The Mayo Clinic suggests that sleeping aids are most effective when used in conjunction with other kinds of treatment, such as cognitive behavioural therapy.[32]

The Affects of Medication on the Liver

While there are different types of medications used for sleeping aids, those that contain acetaminophen are at a high risk for liver problems.[33] This active ingredient is found in sleep medications which also helps with pain relief. So be aware if you are taking medications with this ingredient on a regular basis.

Affects of Medication on Sleep Quality

Sleeping medication in most cases is a temporary solution. Medications can help break patterns of poor sleep, help to fall asleep fast and get some much needed sleep. They do not address the underlying cause and research has shown this time and time again. Researchers have shown that these medications can help you to fall asleep faster but they also contribute to fragmented sleep.[34] The time spent in deep sleep and Rapid Eye Movement (REM) sleep (dreaming) is reduced which can affect your memory and impair your performance.

Safety Concerns

Most medications including sleeping medications carry some form of side effects. However, it is different for everyone and you won't know until you use them. This is why doctors sometimes try you on different medications and different doses until one is found to suit you. Some common known side effects of sleeping medications are:

- Burning or tingling in the hands, arms, feet, or legs
- Changes in appetite
- Constipation/Diarrhoea
- Dizziness and forgetfulness
- Drowsiness
- Dry mouth
- Headaches

There may be other side effects if you have other underlying health problems like Kidney Disease, Asthma or Chronic Obstructive Pulmonary Disease (COPD). Sleeping medications can interfere with breathing so extra caution may be advised by your doctor.[35]

Some people can also be allergic to any of the ingredients in the medication.[36] Some signs of allergic reactions are:

- Blurred vision
- Chest pain
- Difficulty swallowing or breathing
- Rash
- Itching
- Swelling in the face or throat

CHAPTER 6

Sleep and Hormones

The endocrine system is responsible for producing, regulating and distributing hormones, which are chemicals that control cellular functions. These hormones include oestrogen, progesterone, testosterone, adrenaline, cortisol and insulin which are circulated throughout the body. These chemical messengers, when released into the bloodstream, are responsible for growth, metabolising nutrients and overall body function.

There are different types of hormones; lipid-derived, amino acid-derived, and peptide hormones. Most of the lipid hormones are the steroid hormones like testosterone and cortisol. Amino acid hormones are your thyroid hormone, thyroxine and melatonin, the sleep hormone made by the pineal gland. Other amino acid hormones are the adrenal hormones, adrenaline and noradrenaline made from tyrosine and tryptophan which are found in most protein foods. Finally, peptide hormones are the protein molecules like oxytocin and the Human Growth Hormone (HGH).[37]

When you don't get enough sleep, you are directly affecting you circadian biological clock. Hormones are produced and released according to the circadian rhythm. When sleep is deprived, these hormones are not efficient in the bloodstream and can cause a myriad of imbalances in the body.

Sleep Hormones

Melatonin is probably the most known hormone associated with sleep. It is produced as part of the circadian cycle and biological processes. The Human Growth Hormone (HGH) is released during the deep stages of slow wave sleep. This hormone is very important for growth and repair, and also turning fat into muscle mass and thickening the skin in our later years. Other hormones that are important to understand and active when we are asleep are ghrelin and leptin; our hormones that make us feel hungry and full. Other hormones that are active during the day are inhibited at night like cortisol and the Thyroid Stimulating Hormone (TSH). TSH rises in the late evening just before going to bed and starts to decline shortly after sleep going asleep (midnight to 2 am).[38]

How Sleep Hormones are Made

The pineal gland, also known as the 'third eye', responds to light and darkness. Light picked up from the retina in the eye, is relayed to the Suprachiasmatic Nucleus (SCN) of the hypothalamus. The hypothalamus regulates hormones, body temperature and other functions helping to regulate our sleep/wake cycle. Melatonin is a sleep hormone made in response to darkness and the sleep/wake cycle. Serotonin, a neurotransmitter, which is derived from the amino acid tryptophan, is the precursor to melatonin. Shift work and jet lag are probably two of the most know problems contributing to low levels of melatonin resulting in difficulty getting to sleep.

Thyroid Function

Thyroid is a small butterfly shaped glands in the throat which produces thyroid hormones, regulating our metabolism, weight, growth, heart rate, body temperature, fertility, energy levels. It also regulates brain development in the Central Nervous System (CNS) and regulates the Autonomic Nervous System (ANS) which is our 'fight or flight' and 'rest and digest' systems. We also need thyroid function for our Basil Metallic Rate (BMR) for oxygen consumption to produce energy in our cells known as Adenosine

Triphosphate (ATP).[39] Your thyroid also produces a hormone that controls the amount of calcium in the blood.[40] The hypothalamus secretes Thyrotropin-Releasing Hormone (TRH) to the pituitary gland and from there, the pituitary gland secretes TSH. This then causes the thyroid to produces two hormones, Thyroxine (T4) and Triiodothyronine (T3). Iodine is required to make these hormones. Thyroid hormones are lipid in nature so they need to bind to thyroid binding proteins which allow them to be transported in the bloodstream. There is usually more T4 produced than T3, yet T3 is more active. So when T4 arrives at the target site, it is converted to T3.

Hyperthyroidism is excessive amounts of thyroid hormones causes by an autoimmune condition called Graves Disease. Antibodies bind to the TSH, blocking it and causing your thyroid to produce more thyroid hormones. Sometimes this can swell up into what is called a Goitre. Signs and symptoms of Hyperthyroidism are weight loss, increased appetite, sleeping problems, anxiety and sensitivity to heat. You feel jittery and you just can't relax. Hyperthyroidism causes the nervous system to be overactive causing anxiety and a rapid pulse. This can interfere with sleep when the body needs to slow down in preparation for sleep. Some other signs that this could be a contributing factor are night sweats, feeling cold and tired. Thyroid disease is often overlooked because thyroid function affects cellular activity all over the body. See your doctor and ask for a blood test to check thyroid levels if nothing else is obvious to you that is making you tired during the day.

Hypothyroidism is when too little amounts of thyroid hormones are being made caused by an autoimmune condition called Hashimoto's Disease which damages the thyroid itself. This causes the pituitary to make more TSH in an effort to make more thyroid hormones. This can also cause the area to swell up causing a Goitre. Signs and symptoms of hypothyroidism are as fatigue, feeling cold, low blood pressure and weight gain. Hypothyroidism slows everything down and you feel like you want to sleep all the time, even during the day.

Some common causes of thyroid diseases are:

- If it runs in the family
- Too little iodine in the diet
- Exposure to radiation in the neck/throat area i.e. radiation treatments[41]

Fluoride is a known neurotoxin which affects our brain development from a young age and also our thyroid health.[42] Our tap water contains fluoride which is an endocrine disrupter and contributes to Hypothyroidism and Attention Deficit Hyperactivity Disorder (ADHD). Most of the fluoride added to our water contains heavy metals and toxic chemicals like lead and arsenic.[42] Chlorophyll will remove heavy metals including lead, mercury and arsenic.[43]

Selenium (Brazil nuts) is essential in converting Thyroxine to its active form, T3. Eat Cruciferous vegetables like broccoli, kale and spinach as these contain high amounts of phytonutrients to help boost glutathione levels to balance hormones and restore thyroid function.[44] If you have Hashimoto's, avoid gluten.

Studies show that gluten stimulates thyroid anti-body production.[45]

Disruptions in the Hormonal System

Behaviours and Emotions

We can go from feeling happy to sad and anxious in a matter of a few seconds. This can change our emotions and how we hold our body physically, our posture. This happens as a result of chemical reactions in the brain and the body. This lack of control contributes to how we react, respond or behave. However, we do have the ability to regulate and control our emotions.

We can influence the way we perceive a negative situation by how we think. The way we think about things really matters. We interpret and perceive things differently depending on how we are feeling. For example, if we are nervous of an exam or interview coming up, we can prepare ourselves before time. Or maybe you feel uncomfortable and inferior in certain company, feeling not good enough. If something changes from our normal routine or if something is taken away, our behaviour is affected which has an impact on our moods. Take a step back and watch the behaviour. By becoming aware and conscious of the change in behaviour, we can begin to control and master our responses and emotions instead of reacting to them.

Lack of sleep can contribute hugely to our inability to regulate our emotions. We become irritable, angry and grumpy. Sugar cravings set in and we start to have emotional hunger. Our lack of focus and attention is prevalent. You become pessimistic and not optimistic for outcomes and you tend to recall negative memories over pleasant ones. We are unable to be conscious of what is going on. The brain is hard wired to protect us and stopping us from doing anything other that what we know or have already experienced. Our brain doesn't like any kind of change. It sees them as a risk and a risk is dangerous. We just see the negative reactions, we are just confirming and reinforcing what our brain is telling us. Our brain is always trying to protect us but doesn't always serve us when we want to move forward. So we have to work at changing and managing our thought patterns for new outcomes. Bring your thoughts back to your 'why'. What is your motive for doing what you want to do and what is the fear that's holding you back? What is your desire and what is it that you believe in for this to be important to you. This is possible when we have a clear and focused mind but not when we are sleep deprived or lacking in sleep.

At night when we can't sleep, our emotions can really play havoc. It can start when it's time to go to bed. Before you even hit the pillow, your stomach is in a knot. You get frustrated and very quickly resign to the fact that you just won't sleep. You toss and turn and get even more annoyed. You start to direct this anger at your soundly sleeping partner and a feeling of jealousy arises. At this stage, it just feels hopeless and you have a feeling of despair and loneliness. If this type of behaviour continues regularly, it can lead to depression and start to fuel deeper and darker emotions from past experiences in your life adding to your already exasperating problem.

The very act of fighting against these anticipated emotions gives them strength to become so overwhelming and leaving you feeling absolutely exhausted. If you can become aware of these thoughts and feelings and welcome them in, allow them to be there, then there will be no resistance and you don't get caught up in them.

Common Hormonal Imbalances

70% of women and men have some sort of hormonal imbalance. The most common are Hypothyroidism (40%) which includes Hashimoto's, that's the auto-immune form where the anti-body blocks TSH stimulations. Also other hormonal imbalances are infertility, Premenstrual Syndrome (PMS), high oestrogen levels (causes Polycystic Ovaries (PCOS) and endometriosis), menopause symptoms and hot flushes, low testosterone/impotence and high Dihydroxtestosterone (DHT) which causes baldness and prostate issues in men.[46]

Oestrogen Dominance

There are 16 different oestrogens in the body. However, 3 of them are most relevant: oestrone (E1), oestradiol (E2) and oestriol (E3) (protective).[47] The one that tends to give us problems is oestradiol (E2). It's the one responsible for multiple cell production and in relation to cancer. We need to have a balance of oestradiol and progesterone. The 2/16 hydroxyestrone Test is a test of metabolites of oestrogen. You can do a saliva or urine test with your naturopath or functional medicine doctor. In the blood you are looking at the total value of the hormone. The ranges are usually very broad.[48]

The worse characteristics of oestrogen are that they switch on a gene called the BCL2 gene (a cancer gene). This then causes cells to multiply. If this condition is not balanced by adequate levels of progesterone, it can lead to cancer, if the immune system is compromised. Progesterone switches off the BCL2 gene and switches on a protective gene P53, which gives the right message to the cells and protects against cancer.[49] They then mature, differentiate and die and are thereby replaced by other healthy cells. When oestrogen is not balanced with its antagonist, progesterone, it gives rise to this dangerous state of excess oestrogen which, in turn, produces many distressing symptoms referred to as 'Oestrogen dominance'. These vary from Premenstrual Syndrome (PMS) , infertility caused from Endometriosis, Fibroids and Polycystic Ovarian Syndrome (PCOS) and low sperm count in men to increased cancer risks, depression, heart disease, gallbladder problems, thyroid problems to mention a few.

Progesterone and Stress

Progesterone is the calming hormone and the one that helps us get pregnant. There is an interesting link between progesterone levels in the body and stress. Adrenaline, noradrenaline and cortisol (one of the corticosteroids) all come directly from progesterone. We now demand outputs of stress hormones never experienced in our history before. As it is the survival hormone, our body will produce it before any other hormone. Consequently, due to the high demand, our progesterone levels are sucked dry, leaving not enough to balance the rest. Cortisol, likewise, is a drain on our progesterone levels, as this is the hormone produced when we worry. Deficiencies in the other hormones then lead to early degenerative disease – a lack of corticosteroids results in increased allergies, autoimmune disease, arthritis and other inflammatory conditions. Progesterone can't get into the cells when there is a lot of inflammation. Inflammation comes from stress.

Chakras

Each chakra is associated with specific organs and emotional states, as well as a colour. (The 7 Chakras are the energy centres in our body in which energy flows through.) Each gland from the endocrine system is governed and influenced by the chakra system.

Essential oils can help to balance the chakra centres and the endocrine systems. We all have an electrical frequency which is defined as a measurable rate of electrical energy flow that is constant between any two points. Essential oils contain frequencies that are several times greater than that of herbs and foods. They help us to transform emotions and help to bring the body into a higher state of vibration.

Dr. Robert O. Becker, in his book 'The Body Electric', tells us that the human body has an electrical frequency, and also that much about a person's health can be determined by its frequency levels.

Bruce Taino of Taino Technology, Washington, built the first frequency monitor in the world. It used a highly sensitive sensor to measure bio electrical frequencies of elements in the essential oils. This measures the life force of the oils. Taino has determined that general human healthy frequency is within the range of 62-68 MHz and when at lower levels, a variety of diseases can appear. For example at the level of 58 MHz, diseases like cold and flu appear. At 42 MHz, cancer appeared in many humans.[50]

Negative emotions and thoughts can actually drop our frequency by 15 MHz. Our body stores them in organs and glands of the body at the corresponding frequency. A prayer or positive attitude can also raise our frequency by 15 MHz.

Essential oils frequency starts at 52 MHz and go as high as 320 MHz, which is the frequency of rose oil.

- Root Chakra (1st) — Associated with the reproductive glands (testes in men; ovaries in women); controls sexual development and secretes sex hormones. The colour is red and it rules the emotions of security and trust. Essential oils to help raise this vibration are *Vetiver and Patchouli*.

- Sacral Chakra (2nd) — Associated with the adrenal glands; regulates the immune system and metabolism. The colour is orange and it rules the emotions of desire, creativity and the ability to connect with others. Essential oils to help raise this vibration are *Jasmine, Rose and Sandalwood*.
- Solar Plexus Chakra (3rd) — Associated with the pancreas; regulates metabolism. The colour is yellow and it rules the emotions of empowerment and self-confidence. Essential oils to help raise this vibration are *Lemon, Black Pepper and Juniper.*
- Heart Chakra (4th) — Associated with the thymus gland; regulates the immune system. The colour is green (healing) and pink (love) and it rules the emotions of love, healing and forgiveness. Essential oils to help raise this vibration are *Bergamot, Geranium and Rose*..

Thymus Thump

If you want to boost your immune system, increase your strength and vitality, do the 'thymus thump'. It's a simple technique to help stimulate your energy system. Locate the thymus in the centre of your chest on the sternum bone. Make a fist and thump it. Also called the 'Tarzan spot'.

- Throat Chakra (5th) — Associated with the thyroid gland; regulates the body's metabolism and body temperature. The colour is blue and it rules the emotions of speaking your truth, communications and self-authenticity. Essential oils to help raise this vibration are *Peppermint, Basil and Blue Chamomile.*

The thyroid gland, which controls the body's metabolism, is affected by emotions like frustration and stifled ambition. The throat can be affected by traumas like divorce and bereavement or by unhappy relationships.

- Third Eye Chakra (6th) — Associated with the pituitary gland; master gland and governs the function of the previous five glands. The colour is indigo and it rules the emotions of awareness and insights. Essential oils to help raise this vibration are *Rosemary, Juniper and Lemon.*
- Crown Chakra (7th) — Associated with the pineal gland; regulates biological cycles, including sleep. The colour is violet and it rules the emotions of spirituality and connection to the universe. Essential oils to help raise this vibration are *Frankincense, Jasmine and, Neroli.*
- As well as the endocrine glands, there are also seven layers of light in the retina of the eye, and there are seven colours in the solar spectrum and seven scale steps in a musical octave. All these groups require harmony for happiness and health. If just one endocrine gland is out of step, harmony is lost, and the symphony will not sound very pleasing.
  See Figure 6 The Chakras.

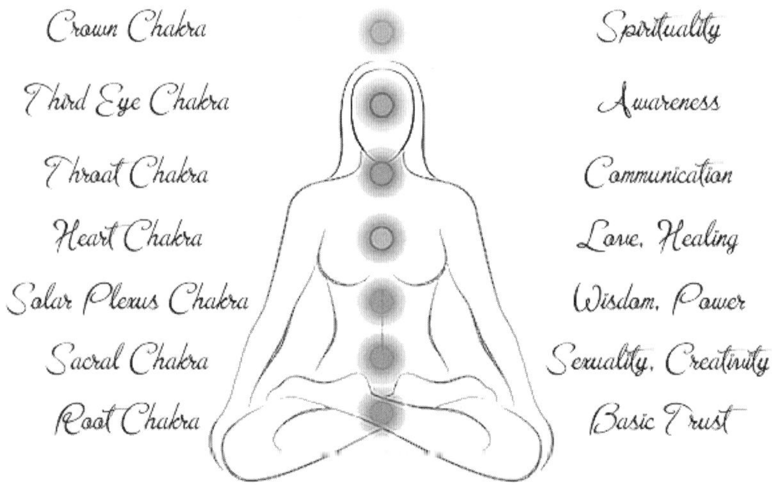

Figure 6 The Chakras

Top 6 Essential Oils

- The 6 best essential oils to naturally balance hormones (adaptogenic).
- **Sage oil** regulates the function of the hypothalamus. It has a beneficial effect on the sweating regulating mechanism which makes it useful for hot flushes experienced in the menopause. In addition, peppermint oil can help cool the body from hot flushes.
- **Clary Sage oil** is used to naturally balance oestrogen's levels. It is the most effective essential oil that offers relief from menopause symptoms like hot flushes.
- **Thyme oil** helps to naturally support progesterone levels. A lot of women in 20's have naturally high oestrogen which starts to drop around the age of 35. Oestrogen levels start to fluctuate dramatically when a women reaches the age of 40. It is particularly important to balance these two hormones. In addition, roman chamomile oil supports progesterone levels by helping to reduce stress with its calming properties.
- **Sandalwood oil** is particularly good for the men. It helps improve libido (low testosterone).
- **Vetiver oil** works directly on the nervous system helping to calm and slow it down. Works great with children with hyper anxiety.
- **Frankincense oil** helps the immune system which affects the hormonal system. Great for thyroid problems.

Primrose oil is known as a carrier oil or vegetable oil and contains GLA (Omega 6). It is used as a base to add essential oils into and to help carry or absorb the essential oils into the body.

Tip: Mix 2 drops of thyme oil and 4 drops of clary sage essential oils into 20mls primrose oil. Rub into the abdomen and soles of the feet. This will help to balance out the oestrogen and progesterone levels.

How to use Essential Oils

Massage Blend — Mix 3 drops of your chosen essential oils into 10mls of carrier oil like almond oil or sunflower oil. Massage into the body.

In a Bath — Put a few drops on some magnesium flakes and drop into a warm bath right before bed.

Inhalation — Add 2 drops of essential oil onto a tissue. You can also inhale straight from the bottle.

Oil Diffuser — Add 7 drops of essential oils to an oil diffuser or candle burner.

Complementary Therapies

Reflexology is a positive effect on the workings of the endocrine and nervous system. The use of essential oils from plants to create harmony for mind, body and soul is yet another way of restoring balance. Another good treatment for hormonal imbalance is Craniosacral Therapy (CST), acupuncture and reiki. Reiki involves drawing down universal energy and guiding it into the chakras in order to release any blockages and allow them to spin at optimum speed. Tapping or Emotional Freedom Technique (EFT) works very well to help release unwanted emotions. Doing this during the daytime, will help reduce the risk of these emotions showing up at night time when there are no distractions.[51] All complementary therapies have one thing in common and that is they help to balance the body, reduce cortisol, the stress hormone, and raising serotonin levels helping to make you feel good also helping to promote sleep.

Diet and Nutrition

Our eating patterns and what we consume can have a significant impact on how we sleep. The biological circadian rhythms are controlled by the master clock in the hypothalamus but also by clocks of peripheral organs. Although the internal master clock in the hypothalamus is strongly controlled by light, clocks of peripheral organs are also influenced by food consumption and patterns, which can reset the biological clock.

Sticking to a regular eating plan could also help to reduce the risk of hearth disease, obesity, Type 2 Diabetes, and stroke.

> ***The American Heart Association has released a statement in the journal 'Circulation' that looks at some of the eating patterns and behaviours that impact on illness.*** [52]

People's eating habits have changed dramatically over the years with most of us skipping breakfast and not consuming three standard meals a day. This affects our body's internal clock and contributing to a restless night's sleep. Also, by eating mindfully, and being aware of what you eat, will help to control unwanted and unconscious emotional eating.

Digestion

When it comes to digestion and hormonal imbalance there are 3 vital areas to look at:

- The health of your digestion
- Sugar levels
- Health of your liver

Digestive Health

If you are having digestive issues you are putting stress on your body. This will cause your cortisol levels to go up and inflammation in the body. This sucks your progesterone dry (the calming hormone), uses vast resources of minerals and vitamins, which increases oxidative cellular stress, free radicals and causes an imbalance in the digestive system. Problems with digestive issues are bloating, gas belching, constipation and stomach aches. Food intolerance will cause leaky gut and huge inflammation. If you are having hormonal imbalance issues get off dairy and gluten firstly. Try gluten free foods or take note of any foods that don't agree with you and eliminate them from your diet. Too many carbohydrates will increase oestrogen and cortisol levels.

Adaptogenic Herbs and Foods

Adaptogenic herbs and supplements can help stabilise blood sugar, improve metabolism, reduce anxiety and support adrenal function.

- Ashwagandha and Holy Basil helps to lower cholesterol, balance cortisol and thyroid T4 levels.
- Rhodiola helps with metabolism and blood sugar levels (Type 2 Diabetics).
- Dong quai (Angelica sinensis) is used for Premenstrual Syndrome (PMS) and menopausal symptoms. It interacts with the blood thinner, warfarin, so seek advice.[53]
- Siberian ginseng, Agnus castus and liquorice root are great for GI Stress (gut health) and emotion stress.

Microbiome

Microorganisms are comprised of bacterial, fungi and viruses and all around us including the water we drink, the food we eat, on our skin and in our gut. Our gut flora is primarily made up of mostly bacteria and the rest is fungi and viruses. With a strong healthy immune system, these bugs coexist with us and don't cause us any problems. Our good bacteria generally help with digestion and keep the bad guys from over multiplying. Fungi include mould and yeast. The most frequent form of fungal infection is candida yeast overgrowth. An overgrowth of candida can result in weakening the gut membrane and lead to leaky gut. If you have regular digestive problems, chances are your have an imbalance of good and bad bacteria in your gut. It is imperative that we look after our gut flora also known as microbiome. 95% of serotonin (the good mood hormone) is made in the gut. It helps make vitamin B12 and short chain fatty acids which are bio-available for the body. Estrobolene, is a bacteria that is responsible for metabolising oestrogen, helping to reduce oestrogen dominance.

The gut-brain axis is responsible for a variety of processes in the body including sleep. It helps to regulate the circadian cycle, the sleep/wake drive and important hormones required for sleep. The microbiome is the key influencer here.

The gut-brain axis is involved in the stress responses between the brain and gut via the vagus nerve, hormone messaging and the immune system. The gut bacteria or microbiome is a key player in this activity. We have 100 trillion microbes in our body. These bacteria, called microbes, outnumber our own cells 10:1.

We know that stress robs the body of vitamins and nutrients and stress also alters or kills our good microbiome. In addition, overuse of antibiotics and environmental toxins contribute to damaging the microbiome. An unbalanced microbiome can contribute to anxiety, depression, and GI disorders (digestive problems) like irritable bowel and colitis. The gut has a major influence on brain function and behaviour.

Stress, anxiety and depression can cause sleep disorders.

Neurotransmitters dopamine, serotonin, melatonin and Gamma Aminobutyric Acid (GABA) are made in the gut and responsible for mood and promoting sleep.

The sleep/drive cycle is controlled by the circadian rhythm and cortisol. If cortisol is disrupted in the gut, or over produced, it will have an impact of sleep.

The Hypothalamic-Pituitary-Adrenal (HPA) Axis activity is regulated in line with the circadian rhythm. The HPA axis is involved in the body's 'stress system', which controls cortisol levels and other stress related hormones. It is generally suppressed or under active in people suffering from CFS or burnout. (*See Chapter 6 - Sleep and Hormones - section on Burnout and Chronic Fatigue.*)

A healthy microbiome ensures the stress response by the adrenals is not over activated, which would otherwise make the adrenals work harder and send excess cortisol into the bloodstream.

An unhealthy microbiome can open the pain gate increasing sensitivity to pain because the communications are impaired between the gut and the brain. Having pain when going to sleep can make falling asleep very difficult.

A healthy diet including probiotics is essential for healthy gut flora, also known as microbiome. Microbial activity is key to normal circadian function, and therefore to sleep. It is also vital for the regulation of weight and metabolism.

Proteins

Protein is vital for energy, weight loss, and sleep. Protein is our building blocks for muscle and tissue repair, neurotransmitter function, balancing blood sugar and brain function amongst an array of other functions. Examples of amino acids are tyrosine, tryptophan, methionine, Gamma Aminobutyric Acid (GABA) and theanine. Theanine can help to slow down brain waves and promote a restful sleep. GABA is a neurotransmitter helping to calm down excitatory neurons allowing the body to slow down in preparation for sleep.

There are 9 essential amino acids that are vital for life but can't be made by the body. These amino acids must be obtained from food which can in turn then make the non-essential amino acids. Amino acids are a very important part of our diet and may help with some health conditions. These include:

- Mood disorders like depression and anxiety
- Sleep disorders
- Comfort and binge eating
- Hyperactivity and learning difficulties

Tryptophan is probably the most effective amino acid required to make serotonin which is our precursor for our sleep hormone, melatonin. It can also help to reduce tension in the body helping to alleviate headaches and migraine. It is a mood balancer since it helps for other hormones to be made. Tryptophan also makes 5-hydroxytryptophan (5HTP) which has been shown to reduce depression symptoms. Eating protein rich foods together with a high glycemic carbohydrate will help tryptophan cross the blood-brain barrier, where it can increase serotonin levels. Examples are potatoes, veggies and beans. This works by excess sugar being produced and therefore insulin, as a result of the high glycemic carbohydrate.

Other proteins are distracted or suppress their activity except for tryptophan. This gives tryptophan a chance to connect with the cell receptors. It should be noted however, a high glycemic index diet is not advised in general because this will send your blood sugar balance out of control. Examples of good sources of tryptophan are turkey, salmon, spirulina, brown rice and chicken.

Healthy Fats

Eating Healthy Fats are the fundamental building blocks for hormonal production and keeping inflammation at bay. Omega 3 fish oil contains Eicosapentaenoic Acid (EPA) and Docosahexaenoic Acid (DHA). Children require DHA for growth and brain development. DHA reduces inflammation and auto-immune reactions while EPA omega-3 has been shown to be most effective for supporting cognitive function, behaviour, mental health, critical for thyroid function, dry skin conditions, asthma and allergies, and regulates our stress responses. Hemp seed and evening primrose contains Gamma Linolenic Acid (GLA) (Omega 6), a natural hormone balancer.

Vitamin D

While vitamin D is formed in the body with the help of sunlight and cholesterol, it can also be obtained through diet and supplements. It is a key factor in hormonal balance and a healthy immune system. It is rich in antioxidant and anti-carcinogen properties and may help to prevent cancer. Vitamin D3 is a pro-hormone. It is adaptive to the immune system, supports insulin secretion by the pancreas, it is necessary for calcium absorption and bone mineralization, regulates blood pressure, supports brain and fetal development, extremely effective to balance hormones. Up to 70% of people with Fibromyalgia and Chronic Fatigue/Burnout (Adrenal Fatigue) have been shown to be deficient in vitamin D3. Kidney disease and increased asthma attacks can occur with deficiencies of vitamin D3. Get 30 minutes of direct sunlight a day while walking.

Sugar Levels

There are many studies to show that people who don't get enough sleep are prone to developing diabetes and heart disease. Sleep affects your blood sugar levels and blood glucose can affect your sleep. It's a vicious cycle. When we don't get enough sleep it affects how we feel the next day including our mood and energy. This also increases stress in the body which increases our cortisol levels which increases our blood sugar. When your blood sugar is high the kidneys try to get rid of it through urination. This will wake you during the night adding to the problem of fragmented sleep. Excessive urination will also lead you to feeling thirsty with a need to drink water during the night. High blood sugar increases your body temperature which is not ideal at night because the body temperature reduces as part of the circadian cycle to help promote active hormones at night.

When we have spikes in blood sugar, it causes a corresponding drop in the blood sugar. If we experience this low drop during the night, adrenaline and cortisol will release into the blood stream in order to raise blood sugar levels. These hormones stimulate the brain and wake us up. Some good bedtime snacks to keep blood sugar stable are oatmeal, wholegrain foods and complex carbohydrates. It is important that the blood sugar levels do not go too high or too low, but to keep them balanced optimally enabling the body to function optimally also.

Artificial Sweeteners

Many people opt for artificial sweeteners for the purpose of weight control. Aspartame is a zero calories sweetener and often contained in sugar free drinks like diet sodas. However, it is important to know that this sweetener is broken down into 3 metabolites: – phenylalanine, aspartic acid and methanol. Phenylalanine is addictive, with its dopamine related effects; maybe that's why so many people like coke and similar drinks. Aspartame is also metabolised to formaldehyde, a neurotoxin. It can decrease levels of serotonin and dopamine in the brain.[54]

Studies have shown that eating artificial sugars can actually make you feel hungry and increase your appetite.

The study published in the journal 'Cell Metabolism' in July 2016, Volume 24 Issue 1, investigated the effect that artificial sweeteners have on the brain. We need sugar for energy; however artificial sweeteners changes our sweet taste and tells the brain that we haven't had enough and so increases our appetite for more energy.[55]

The study links artificial sweeteners with hyperactivity, reduction in serotonin and dopamine and results in poor quality sleep. Artificial sweeteners also have a toll on the liver with it's toxic by products.

Liver Health

Our liver is responsible for eliminating toxic substances out of our body. Toxins come from many different forms like environmental pollution, toxic ingredients in personal care products, emotional stress, hormone metabolites and the foods we eat. The liver eliminates toxins from the body including hormone metabolites and heavy metals. Silver fillings in the teeth can leak mercury into the thyroid. Teflon pans release carcinogenic particles when heated.

Research shows that hormone disrupting chemicals have been linked to a number of health problems including infertility, lower sperm counts, obesity, diabetes, thyroid imbalance, and certain types of cancers. Hormone disruptors come from bisphenol A. BPA (BPA), found in plastic containers that store food and beverages, tricloson (antibacterial soaps and body washes), oxybenzone and dioxins. Avoid personal care products that contain parabens. Toxic ingredients are used to preserve products and make them smell good. The health and beauty industry is a business and many companies will do whatever it takes to make money. Even if this includes using additives and preservatives that are not safe to put on the human body! Many people ignore this because they are only putting these products on their skin and not ingesting them. However, this is not the case.

Did you know that your skin is the largest organ in your body and 60% of EVERYTHING you put ON your skin goes INTO your body!

Toxic overload is obvious when we experience headaches, dizziness, nausea and fatigue. While we can't avoid all toxins, we can become aware of them and reduce the overall accumulated effects.

The Electrical Body

We are primarily made of water and salts which contribute to our electrical activity. Every cell, organ and neuron needs low levels of an electrical current to function. The **electrical activity** of the brain can be monitored by way of an Electroencephalogram (EEG). The heart can by monitored by an Electrocardiogram (ECG/EKG). All humans have a bioelectric field. When an injury or trauma occurs on the skin, it causes a localised shift and disruption in current flow. This in turn causes the brain to react with repair and regeneration instructions. People are constantly taking energy in from the environment including light energy from the sun, oxygen and food. The body uses these outside sources of energy and transforms it in the mitochondria in our cells to an energy source the body can use also known as Adenosine Triphosphate (ATP). Our nervous and endocrine system needs electrical energy to function and enable all other cellular activity. Foods to support these body systems and enable clear electrical systems are fatty acids, vitamin E and minerals.

PMS and Sleep

Different stages of the menstrual cycle have different effects on sleep. The hormones oestrogen and progesterone rise and fall during the menstrual cycle which can affect the quality of sleep. Oestrogen builds up until the woman begins ovulation. On day 14, when the woman begins ovulating, the oestrogen rises again. This is the prime time when women have difficulty around sleep. After ovulation, progesterone, the calming hormone begins to rise. Just before menstruation, oestrogen and progesterone levels drop, which can contribute to more sleeping problems. If there is a gradual change in these hormones, sleep problems are not affected as much. However, it is the dramatic changes in hormone levels that cause difficulties in getting asleep and staying asleep. Avoid excess alcohol and exercise during the day. This will help to promote deep sleep.

Menopause and Sleep

Menopause is a time in a women's life when she stops being reproductive. The ovaries stop producing oestrogen and progesterone and she stops menstruating. This typically happens around the late 40's and early 50's. As part of this process, it can lead to sleeping difficulties. When the oestrogen and progesterone stop producing, it can cause an imbalance in hormonal activity and cause hot flushes and sweats. The drop in oestrogen is what is thought to confuse the hypothalamus (our temperature regulator/thermostat) into thinking the body is overheating which causes the sweat glands to turn on in order to cool the body down. When night time sweats occur, it can make sleeping very difficult. Avoid dehydration and hot drinks at night. Avoid spicy foods which can exasperate the problem. Avoid emotional upset which can increase adrenal activity. A herbal extract of sage can help to keep temperature levels under control.

Kevin Connolly from healthyliving.ie recommends A.Vogel Menoforce Sage tablets.

Exercise and Sleep

Exercise speeds up your metabolism, elevates body temperature, and stimulates hormones such as cortisol and adrenaline. This isn't a problem if you're exercising in the morning or afternoon, but too close to bed and it can interfere with sleep.

Try to finish moderate to vigorous workouts at least three hours before bedtime. If you're still experiencing sleep difficulties, move your workouts even earlier. Relaxing, low-impact exercises such as yoga or gentle stretching in the evening can help promote sleep.

Managing Stress

What is it? Stress is anything that threatens our physical and mental wellbeing. There are many factors affecting our stress including survival, environmental, lifestyle, diet, financial worry, work. It is how an individual responds to any kind of demand. When stress is experienced, chemicals are released into the bloodstream to give more energy and strength. This enables us to cope with physical danger of a physical activity. However, if it is in response to an emotional experience, then there is no outlet for the adrenaline to be used up.

How it Affects the Body

Stress can affect the mind and the body. There are three stages to stress.

First Stage: Adrenaline and corticosteroids are released into the bloodstream increasing the heart rate and breathing. Digestion and the immune system slow down as blood is pumped to the required organs and limbs. Energy is released quickly from stored fats and sugars.

Second Stage: All the extra adrenaline and corticosteroids are used to enable the body to cope. The body is designed to return to normal after the stressful event. However, if the situation is prolonged or continuous, the body enters stage three.

Third Stage: The body becomes exhausted and energy is depleted. Stress affects all our systems which in turn can lead to many symptoms including: reproductive problems, respiratory problems, allergies, insomnia, high blood pressure, indigestion, Irritable Bowel Syndrome (IBS) and low immune system. There tends to be an increase in the consumption of alcohol, cigarettes and sugar as a means of coping.

Essential oils I would use in the treatment of stress:

- ***Roman Chamomile (Chamaemelum nobile) – to help sooth and calm the nervous system.***
- ***Eucalyptus (Eucalyptus Smithii) – for mental exhaustion and clarity.***
- ***Frankincense (Boswellia carteri) – acts as a sedative to balance, easing depression.***
- ***Geranium (Pelargonium graveolens) – to help overcome emotional problems related to the hormones.***
- ***Lavender (Lavandula angustifolia) – to help relax and aid sleep.***
- ***Ylang Ylang (Cananga odorata) – soothing and sensual to help ease anxiety and depression and aid in sleep.***

The primary reasons for sleeping problems are stress, followed by illness, inactivity, medications, and bad sleep environment. 90% of all illnesses and diseases are stress related. High levels of stress hormones not only have a negative impact on the body but also on the brain. When we can't sleep, we can get anxious. Cortisol, the stress hormone, is released into the blood stream. When there are excess amounts, cortisol can break down collagen in the skin, the protein that keeps skin smooth and elastic. This contributes to ageing. Excess cortisol makes the body more vulnerable to pathogens in the body and weakening the immune system. It can lead to a host of problems from weight gain, digestive problems, heart disease, stroke, high blood pressure and diabetes.

CHAPTER 7

Sleep for Anxiety and Depression

Sleep deprivation is usually the result of not being able to fall asleep, difficulty staying asleep, waking too early in the morning, or waking up feeling unrefreshed.

Stress or anxiety can contribute hugely to a sleepless night and sleep disorders. Sleep disorders can be described as abnormal sleep patterns that interfere with physical, mental, and emotional functioning and leaving the body as a whole, out of balance. Stress or anxiety affects the nervous system which in turn affects all other body systems.

When you feel threatened, your nervous system responds by releasing steroid stress hormones, adrenaline and cortisol, into the bloodstream. These stress hormones get your body ready for the 'fight or flight' response. Your heart pounds faster, muscles tighten, blood pressure rises, breath quickens, and your senses become sharper.

Maintaining homeostasis is achieved by managing different stress conditions with the help of central nervous system (through neurotransmitter), endocrine system (through hormones) and immune system (through antibodies). All the three major systems work in synchrony to regulate the body function smoothly. All of these stresses can contribute to disrupting our homeostasis which will require us to adapt some stress management techniques to bring us back to balance.

Anxiety

90% of people are suffering unnecessarily and this is causing persistent levels of stress. Most people with anxiety just can't get to sleep. You lie in bed starring at the ceiling, getting more and more frustrated because you can't go to sleep. When you are in the quite of the night, there are no distractions and so you are alone with your thoughts. You mind is racing with thoughts and it feels like it's going to explode. This is typical most nights going to bed. So for some, before you even get to the bedroom, you are already worried that you won't be able to go to sleep. This brings up fears around sleep and more anxiety.

Some of the symptoms associated with anxiety are:

- A fast heart rate.
- The sensation of having a 'thumping heart' (palpitations).
- Feeling sick (nausea).
- Shaking (tremor).
- Sweating.
- Dry mouth.
- Chest pain.
- Headaches.
- Fast breathing.

People with anxiety often have low serotonin levels and other endorphins. This can result in emotional hunger and cravings in the afternoon and evening. The GABA neurotransmitter counteracts the excitatory neurotransmitter glutamate and this is often low in people with anxiety.[56]

Physical symptoms are a result of messages sent from the brain down through the nervous system making the heart and lungs work faster. In addition, stress hormones are released into the bloodstream enabling this to happen. This brings the body into a 'fight or flight' response.

Anxiety is normal in a stressful situation. For example, having an argument with someone you love or if you are doing a very important exam.

The problem is how we respond to it and that depends on a number of factors. For example, it could be something minor but if we are subjected to this stressful situation regularly without resolution then we will experience anxiety very easily, sometimes without even realising it.

An anxiety disorder usually is the result of a childhood trauma whether it's abusive or losing a parent, or a major stressful event in your life: – losing your home to a fire or a terrible car accident leaving you fighting for your life. The stressful symptoms continue long after the event. The feelings you experience are attached to your past traumatic event which enhances your current stressful situation.

A person with an anxiety disorder usually experiences anxiety most days and can be triggered for the simplest reason.[57] If you have an anxiety disorder then you will be fearful, worried and tense quite a lot of the time. You may experience panic attacks or phobias when feelings of terror overwhelm you and you feel like you are going to die.[58] It can be quite disabling and seriously affect your mental health. If you feel you may be suffering from an anxiety disorder, seek help from your doctor.

Cognitive Behavioural Therapy (CBT) is one good way to help overcome anxiety. Cognitive therapy looks at how we think about things, our thoughts and perceptions and how that makes us react. We can learn to become aware of these thoughts that make us feel anxious. As we become aware of our feelings, we can change how we react and learn to respond with intention and have control over our actions.

Exercise can help because it increases our natural producing endorphins helping us to feel good. Talking to someone can also help and there are a lot of self care books, articles and DVD's that can help too.

Antidepressant medication may be advised by your doctor to help ease symptoms and relax the nervous system.

Anxiety is a stress response and can rob the body of nutrients, causing hormonal imbalance and also have an impact on gut health and the microbiome. Cut down on stimulants like caffeine and reduce your intake of refined carbohydrates, sugar and other processed foods.

Probiotics help to build good bacteria, reducing inflammation in the body and keeping the immune system strong. If the gut lining is broken down or impeded, foreign invaders can get in causing havoc in the gut resulting in irritable bowel, colitis, allergies and autoimmune responses. The microbiome (good bacteria) are responsible for producing the feel good neurotransmitter, serotonin. Probiotics don't last long in the gut so eating prebiotics will help to feed the probiotics, helping them live longer. Prebiotics consist of soluble fibre such as fruit and vegetables and beans. Avoid overuse of antibiotics, because they kill all bacteria, good and bad. Be aware of using acid blockers for reflux because this reduces the production of stomach acid or Hydrochloric Acid (HCL), which can kill parasites and other pathogens that come into the body with the food we eat. We also need stomach acid to digest and absorb our B vitamins.

Goat yogurt, fermented foods, keifer or probiotic supplements and of course don't forget to eat your prebiotics. These act like the fertiliser for your good bacteria and help them to thrive. You might need to get rid of the bad guys first before you start by detoxing. Eating fermented foods may aggravate the problem if you have candida (overgrowth of yeast). In this case you will probably have Small Intestinal Bacterial Overgrowth (SIBO). This will be evident if you produce gas and bloating after eating them.

Depression

Our nervous system, endocrine system and immune system all work in synchronicity to minimise stress situations or the 'fight or flight' response. Stress can be experienced on a physical level, spiritual, emotional and mental level.

When we are constantly tired, it has an impact on our physical health but it also has a huge impact on our mental health. The Central Nervous System (CNS) consists of the brain and the spinal cord. Neurotransmitters, part of the nervous system, travel from one neuron (nerve cell) to another between synapses.
See Figure 7 The Synapse.

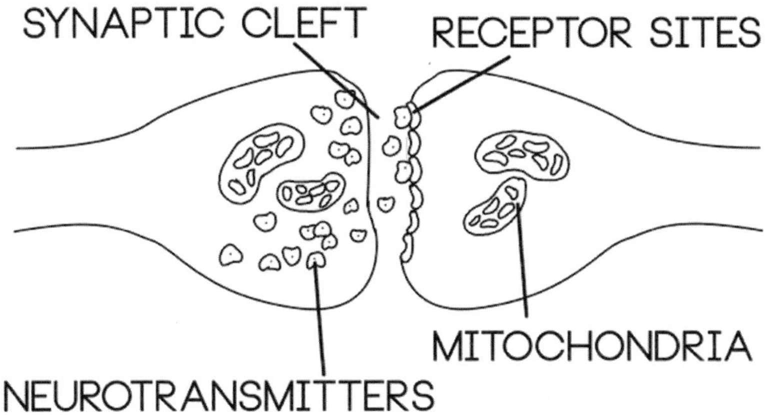

Figure 7 The Synapse

Neurotransmitters bind to certain receptors and will do one of two things. It will do something in an excitatory response, or it will prevent something from happening with an inhibitory response.[59] The brain sends out nerve impulses which communicate with the rest of the body. Sedatives are often used to help slow down the nervous system of an anxious person, helping them to relax or sleep. Overuse of drugs or alcohol, can slow the nervous system down enough to cause depression. When the nervous system is too slow, like when we are depressed, it can cause problems. It interferes with all our bodily systems, having an impact on our digestion, immune system and cardiovascular and our brain function.

We all get a little depressed and feeling down from time to time. However, if over a long period of time, you are continually feeling down, guilty, have difficulty focusing or sleeping, no interest in anything and continually tired, then you should seek help from your doctor. If you find you are sleeping too little or over sleeping on a regular basis, be sure to mention that also. Ongoing altered sleep patterns are an indicator of mental health issues. There is lots of online information and talks that can provide help around understanding this disorder.[60] Depression is a serious disorder and it affects the way a person behaves, thinks and feels including sleeping. Some people use drugs or alcohol to numb or escape feelings. For some, depression is the cause of not sleeping and for others not sleeping is the cause of depression. It has been show over and over that people with chronic sleep deprivation are 10 times more likely to have depression. Clinical studies show that Sleep Apneoa may be linked to depression. People with depression were found to be five times more likely to have Sleep Apneoa.[61] Other sleep studies in depressive patients show that they have less deep sleep and REM sleep.[62]

Inflammation, bad gut flora and a weak immune system can contribute hugely to depression. Chronic stress causes excess cortisol in the body and the brain. This leads to inflammation and a surplus of the neurotransmitter glutamate which in turn leads to free radicals, damaging and even killing brain cells. Excess inflammation can lead to depression and possibly an over active immune system resulting in an autoimmune disease. If there is an over active immune system, the patient is less likely to respond to antidepressants. Therefore, a high percentage of people taking medication, aren't getting any benefit from them.[63] So keeping a strong immune system and a healthy gut is vital.

Studies show that when you experience chronic stress the brain's electrical activities increase in the amygdala and your emotions strengthen. Also, the area in the brain for learning, the hippocampus, weakens.[64]

The Limbic and Olfactory Systems

The olfactory system is part of the sensory system, namely our sense of smell. Our sense of smell is heightened during sleep and the olfactory nerve cells are the only nerve cells which regenerate throughout life.

During inhalation the olfactory system can detect molecules, identify millions of odorants and remember them.

Olfactory receptor neurons are bathed in the mucus produced by the bowman's glands, in the upper nasal sinuses. Hair like cilia, project the receptor cells. The axons of the cells are bundled in villa and project through the bone at the front of the skull. The olfactory bulb lies at the other side of that bone. When inhalation takes place, the odour dissolves in the mucous layer and binds with the receptor cells. The trigger signal is sent to the olfactory bulb and up to the limbic system in the brain. The olfactory bulb in turn sends the impulses to the amygdala. It's directly involved with emotional well-being, the 'fight or flight' response and fear conditioning. This part of the brain stores and releases emotional trauma. The only way to effectively stimulate this gland is with the sense of smell. The olfactory system is the only human sense that bypasses the thalamus which is why it is so quick and effective.

The limbic system and hypothalamus are connected to the part of the brain that controls our nervous system, heart rate, blood pressure, memory and hormones. This is sometimes called the 'emotional brain' as the odours can sometimes trigger emotions such as rage, fear, happiness etc, and causing physiological and psychological effects. The hypothalamus plays an important role in regulating the bodies systems when in stress. Essential oils have a major effect therefore in heightened emotional states such as grief and sadness. *See Figure 8 The Olfactory System.*

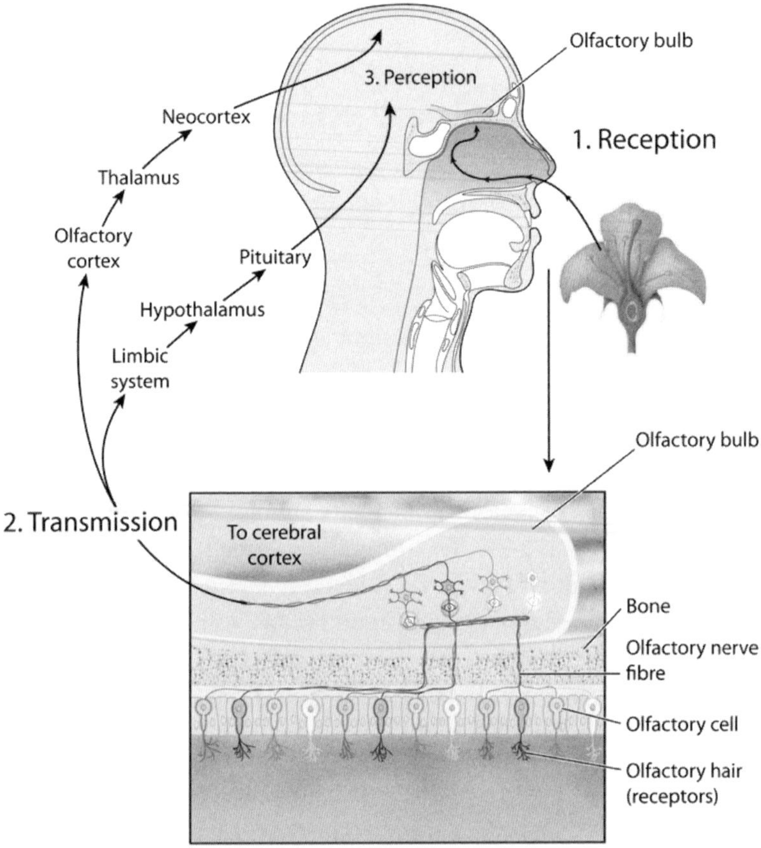

Figure 8 The Olfactory System

Grief

When you are mourning something or the loss of a loved one, you feel torn apart. It can literally feel like your heart is broken. It can leave you feeling physically and emotionally exhausted and leave your spirits in disarray. We often feel numb because our body is in shock and doesn't quite know how to deal with it. This numbness is a protection mechanism so as not to overwhelm us with all the emotions at the same time.

We are all familiar with the 5 stages of grief:

Denial – We are in a state of shock. Our feelings are numb which keeps us safe from the overwhelming feelings. Denial and shock helps us to cope and survive.

Anger – This is when our feelings begin to emerge and it is the start of the healing process.

Bargaining – We will do anything not to feel the pain of the loss of our loved one, so we say things like "Please God," or "I'll never do that again".

Depression – This is when we feel there is no hope, in depths of despair. We start to realise that our loved one is not coming back.

Acceptance – We realise and accept that our loved one is gone. We begin to learn how to live with this reality.

It is a process and we need time, whatever that is for you, to get through them all. People will often tell you, "keep going", "move on from it", "put it behind you" and similar messages like that. When we are grieving, it is so important to mind ourselves, nurture ourselves and slow right down. This is a huge loss and we need to be with our feelings and not run away from them as painful as they are.

Having lost my daughter Megan on the day she was due, I have experienced and learned a great deal. She was perfect, nothing was wrong with her at all. It was a simple cord accident. I remember her last kick only a few hours before we were told there was no heart beat at the hospital. Not being able to sleep was so debilitating for me. I was so desperate at times to just be able to sleep for one whole night.

You see, when we lose someone dear to us, we feel like we have lost some control. When it comes to sleep, we let go of our control in order to sleep. In the case of grief, on a subconscious level, we do not want to let go of any more control.

For me, I had to learn to love myself again, to forgive myself, practice compassion and know that I deserve the very best in life.

Seasonal Affect Disorder (SAD)

SAD occurs mainly in the winter time, often referred to as 'The Winter Blues'. This is affected by hormones and neurotransmitters namely, serotonin, dopamine, melatonin and noradrenaline.

- Rhodiola is an adaptogen herb helping to boost brain power. It has been shown to help improve brain health, fight low moods and improve focus.
- Low levels of vitamin D have been linked to depression so supplementing with this can help.
- Omega 3 fatty acids have been shown to help improve brain health, depression and anxiety.
- Exercise helps produce endorphins including tryptophan which is required for serotonin.
- Using a light box can help to produce vitamin D levels in the body. The light box can cause chemical changes in the brain helping to improve mood.

Essential oils can help increase the 'feel good' neurotransmitter serotonin by using calming and relaxing oils like lavender, chamomille, marjoram, clary sage or bergamot. Many people who are deficient in serotonin often experience SAD.

Dopamine is another calming neurotransmitter responsible for our emotions and the ability to experience both pleasure and pain. It is when we experience rewards and joy in our life.

Studies have shown that people with a deficiency in dopamine, affects poor eating habits or emotional eating (food cravings). It also worsens the symptoms of SAD.

Stress Robs your Vitamins and Minerals

It is important to remember that 'stress' can refer to an emotional response or physical stress in the body i.e. cellular oxidative stress from free radicals. Free radicals are a normal result of cellular metabolism from the foods we eat or it could be from other environmental pollutants.

Along with other stress management strategies, our vitamins and minerals intake play an important role on minimising stress in our body.

Vitamins and minerals work together and often if we are deficient in one the body does not function optimally as a whole.

Vitamins A, C, and E are powerful anti-oxidants. They help to mop up free radicals which are a result of metabolic process in our bodies.[65] Free radicals can cause a lot of cellular damage throughout our body. It is always a good idea to keep our anti-oxidant levels up by taking supplements or eating foods high in vitamin A, C and E to help keep our free radicals at bay.

The B vitamins, for example thiamine (B1), riboflavin (B2), niacin (B3), pantothenic acid (B5), pyridoxine (B6), and biotin (B7) all work together and are known as co-workers because they help each other. Vitamin B12 and folate (B9) are important in creating healthy DNA, our genetic code. Also, very high levels of homocysteine (a toxic amino acid) are indicators of folate (B9) and B12 deficiency which can lead to many diseases. Homocysteine is a naturally occurring amino acid produced as part of the methylation process in the body. Methylation in very simple terms is when the body changes the structure of a cell enabling it to be bio available or breaking it down for the detoxification process. People who have high levels of homocysteine often eat a lot of red meat. It is important that we can metabolise homocysteine and rid them out of the body or recycled back into methionine. To do this, we need sufficient amounts of vitamins B6, folate (B9) and B12. Homocysteine is a key marker in many illnesses and diseases like Type 2 Diabetes, migraines, heart disease, high cholesterol, and it is also linked to Alzheimer's and Dementia.[66] There are different types of cholesterol; Low-density Lipoprotein (LDL) and High-density Lipoprotein (HDL). High levels of the 'bad' cholesterol, LDL, build up in the walls of your arteries making them hard and narrow. The HDL is the 'good' cholesterol which carries excess cholesterol back to the liver to be broken down.

Any kind of physical or emotional stress robs the body of vitamins especially B vitamins. Too much animal protein, sugar, excess alcohol and caffeine all deplete B vitamins and contribute to a rise in homocysteine levels. The carbon monoxide from cigarette smoke also depletes vitamin B6. Stomach acid is required to absorb B12. Acid blockers can reduce stomach acid, reducing the absorption of B12. Probiotics promotes good bacteria in our gut which help with the absorption of vitamins.

Vitamin K is an important player in blood clotting, preventing excessive bleeding when we have a cut or wound. [67] This works together with the collagen promoted by vitamin C helps which then contributes in forming new tissue to close wounds.[68] Vitamin C is also important for collagen formation which is critical to the health of our skin, tendons, and ligaments. Vitamin D also has a helping hand since this is a big part of the immune system.

When we are in stress mode, 'fight or flight', our body releases steroid hormones which has an effect on our salt and water balance. Minerals like potassium and sodium can build up causing high blood pressure and inflammation. In turn calcium and magnesium become deficient. 85% of people are deficient in magnesium, our natural tranquiliser and muscle relaxant. Bananas are probably one of the top foods rich in magnesium. Spinach and kale are also good sources. Chromium is another important mineral that we need to work with insulin, helping the cells absorb glucose. Many people, who experience on going emotional stress or a tragic event, may develop problems with sugar imbalance.[69] Zinc is also required to store insulin.

Hormonal Imbalance

Stress in our modern environment can influence the level of hormones secreted in the body. An over or under production can result in diseases like Graves, Hashimoto's or Addison's Disease. Catecholamines are hormones made mostly by the adrenal glands like adrenaline, noradrenaline, and dopamine. They are released into the bloodstream when under physical or emotional stress. Glucocorticoids, cortisol, helps the body respond to stress but also environmental changes which is prevalent in the circadian cycle. Glucocorticoids are probably the most essential hormones for our survival and therefore it always takes precedence. Stress has an impact of hormonal changes and therefore an impact on the endocrine system. Other hormones affected are thyroid hormones, insulin, Human Growth Hormone (HGH), prolactin (which produces breast milk).[70] Luteinizing Hormone (LH) and Follicle-Stimulating Hormone (FSH) are called gonadotropins because they stimulate the gonads; the testes in males and the ovaries in females.[71] These hormones in turn are also responsible for the production of the sex hormones, testosterone, progesterone and oestrogen.

Oestrogen and progesterone are two of the primary female hormones that balance each other in the body. Excess oestrogen can lead to weight gain and other abnormalities or imbalances. The liver detoxifies excess oestrogen. Good bacteria bind to the oestrogen helping to transport it out of the system as a waste product. When this is not functioning optimally, it is typically because the good bacteria are not binding to the oestrogen. As a result, the oestrogen is recycled and becomes more potent in the system and therefore more dangerous leading to oestrogen based cancers like breast and ovarian cancer. When there is oestrogen dominance, it contributes to difficulties losing weight, Premenstrual Syndrome (PMS) symptoms like cramps, feeling emotional and moody. It promotes weight gain and makes it more difficult to build muscle.

How our Mindset can help

The endocrine system is closely related to the body's own energy system. You are what you eat (absorb) and you are what you think. Every thought influences your body chemistry.

Negative thoughts and feelings such as jealousy, fear or hatred result in blockages in the body's energy system.

How we think contributes significantly to how we feel, our behaviours and actions. Ask yourself, how am I feeling? What's my mood? What's my emotion? How you feel affects what happens to you! Life is a game. You set the rules and play by the rules. Know what your values are and what is important to you. Be certain about what it is you want in life. When you create a level of certainty, negative people will back away from you. Ask yourself what can I do to get closer to what it is I want? Focus on your outcome. What is your dominant thought? What are you focused on? Always lean towards positive thinking and you will have positive results. Our mindset is like playing a game. We are hardwired for the negative stuff that is why it is hard work leaning towards the positive stuff. However, it gets easier with practice. When people get in the way, we are giving away our control and power. We are allowing them to affect our certainty. Protect your mind, your thoughts and mental health. Be the best that you can and that's the very best you can do. You can't be perfect, only the best and you will always improve.

Take part in stress management courses, self help books, cd's, DVD's, relaxation techniques and meditation. Medications and supplements are always an option. Be bigger than your problem. Feelings and emotions are the end product of past experiences. You remember experiences because you remember how you feel. You need to think greater than how you feel; otherwise you are living in the norm. This is what you are used to.

It is also true that our bodies change our minds and our minds change our behaviour and our behaviour changes our outcome. Let your last thought be something that you are thankful for/grateful for.

The Midlife Crisis

This is when people begin to wake up or the soul becomes awakened. Be mindful that soul loss occurs mainly around the midlife period. This is defined as 'a loss of self-confidence and feeling of anxiety or disappointment that can occur in early middle age'. It was first identified by the psychologist Carl Jung and is a normal part of the maturing process. It is a time of emotional transition where some life adjustments need to be made or healing from the past. There is a deep yearning for some time to follow the essence of the soul. These can be major or simple.

The Affects of Sugar

Primarily our blood sugar balance is critical to the overall functioning of our body's systems. Cortisol is responsible for our body's blood sugar levels and thus regulating metabolism, acting as an anti-inflammatory, controlling salt and water balance, influencing blood pressure. If we have too much sugar or starchy foods, a stressful job and don't exercise our blood sugar becomes unbalanced. This in turn leads to hormonal imbalance effecting the production of melatonin (the sleep hormone) and other hormones synthesis. This in turn will affect the brain's neurotransmitters and their functioning. This will affect your mood, making you depressed while the adrenals will kick in from all the stress making you wired and tired. You will be less able to focus and concentrate and become irritable and anxious. Cortisol (the stress hormone) levels rise, which releases more glucose into the bloodstream. The body produces more insulin to tackle the glucose in the blood which ends up causing low blood sugar. With all this stress in the body the serotonin (happy neurotransmitter) is robbed and leads to low serotonin. This is when we crave for sweet foods as a quick fix to raise blood sugar levels and energy and so the whole cycle continues. It's a vicious circle.

The Affects of Cortisol

Cortisol is a naturally occurring steroid hormone that is controlled by the hypothalamus and pituitary gland and secreted by the adrenal glands. This is called the Hypothalamic-Pituitary-Adrenal (HPA) Axis. Cortisol has a variety of functions including metabolism, regulating energy and the immune response. Cortisol is naturally high in the mornings and reduces in the evening time, part of the circadian cycle, in sync with night time and going to sleep. It is also involved in the regulation of your sleep/wake homeostasis cycle and is also produced with adrenaline, in response to stress as part of the 'fight or flight' response. In our fast paced society, the problem now is that we are continually pumping out cortisol in response to stressors. Imbalanced cortisol levels within the body can cause symptoms of excessive tiredness or fatigue resulting in feeling irritable, moody and sensitive to emotions. Prolonged stress can manifest into physical symptoms: - headaches, back ache, joint pain. However, these continued demands will have a detrimental effect on our overall health leading to heart disease, stroke, diabetes and a host of other health problems.

Cortisol inhibits insulin which causes glucose to be stored as fat, which in turn can contribute to weight gain. In the mean time this causes the pancreas to work harder, producing more insulin, however, the cells are insulin resistant leaving more glucose in the bloodstream. It becomes a vicious cycle. The cells can't get the glucose into them so hunger signals are sent to the brain. This causes overeating and so more excess glucose is stored as fat.

Another function that cortisol has is on the immune system and inflammation. If you have a lot of inflammation in the body, it will turn on more of the steroid hormone causing even more inflammation and suppressing the immune system even further. This can lead to more colds and flu, inability to fight off infections, allergies and eventually auto-immune diseases.

Our nervous system is divided into two parts, the sympathetic nervous system and the parasympathetic nervous system. Only one can be activated at a time. Our digestive system belongs to the parasympathetic nervous system, otherwise known as the 'rest and digest' system. Cortisol activates the sympathetic nervous system, and so the digestive system is suppressed when we are in a state of stress. When we eat food in a state of stress, it is not digested and absorbed efficiently. Some common digestion disorders are irritable bowel syndrome and colitis.

Cortisol constricts blood vessels so over time this can lead to problems with high blood pressure and blood vessel damage and a strain on the heart. Over time this can lead to heart disease and a heart attack.

Probiotics in your diet combined with relaxation techniques will help to reduce inflammation, stress hormones and in turn help to reduce weight. In order to have a strong immune system, your gut has to be functioning at an optimal rate. Probiotics help to populate your gut with good bacteria which in turn also produce our neurotransmitters. 95% of serotonin is made in the gut. Our brain requires these neurotransmitters. Neurotransmitters work with receptors in our brains to produce thoughts, feelings and actions. With an imbalance or absence of these neurotransmitters and brain chemicals, we would experience anger, lack of sleep, irritability, anxiety, depression, instability and fear, not to mention the constant release of adrenaline which causes High Blood Pressure (HBP), heart disease, high cortisol, Type 2 Diabetes and more.

To help balance excess cortisol, we must be mindful of stress management. Try some relaxation techniques along with eating anti-inflammatory foods, good fats (omega 3 and 6), less refined carbohydrates and sugary snacks. A little exercise or movement will help the circulation, delivering nutrients to the cells and waste removal process in the body. Include fibre, antioxidants and phytonutrients with fruits, vegetables, nuts and seeds. A diet high in fibre has been linked to lower body weight. Fermentable fibres (prebiotics) are known to affect the important intestinal microbiome.[72]

The Vagus Nerve

People who have anxiety or fatigue normally have a low functioning vagus nerve. The vagus nerve is part of the parasympathetic nervous system and it controls the heart, lungs and the digestive system. In fact, it has an influence on the functioning of all the major organs and involuntary muscles in the body. It is the longest cranial nerve in the body and one of the communication channels for the gut-brain axis. It runs from the brain, the face and down to the stomach and abdomen.

When the vagus nerve is stimulated, it activates the parasympathetic nervous system or otherwise known as the 'rest and digest' system. It calms everything down allowing the body to go into homeostasis and brings the body back into balance. It does this by regulating the adrenal glands and hormonal secretions, digestive flow and all the automatic visceral organ activities. This in turn, dramatically helps to reduce inflammation and controls glucose balance in the blood, reducing the risk of Type 2 Diabetes and the onset of other diseases in the body.

The vagus nerve relationship to the immune system is very important for controlling inflammation. Inflammation is a vital part of the immune system to repair or heal after a blow to the area or an infection. When the immune system over reacts and becomes out of control, this can result in chronic inflammation and long term can lead to auto-immune diseases.

Vagus nerve stimulation can help with a multitude of problems affecting your sleep including anxiety and discontentment. The vagus nerve contributes to how we are feeling and our mental wellbeing. It is part of the mind body connection since it is connected from the brain right down to the abdomen.

Reflux commonly keeps us awake when we lie down. The vagus nerve helps control the production of stomach acid and also controls the involuntary muscles of the oesophagus.

Chanting, singing, laughing and gargling water can all stimulate the vagus nerve. Massages around the neck area are also quite effective. When we hug, we release the oxytocin hormone which is responsible for our social bonding and feeling loved. This hormone in turn also activates the vagus nerve. Yoga, meditation and deep belly breathing are also very effective ways to stimulate the vagus nerve. *See Figure 9 The Vagus Nerve.*

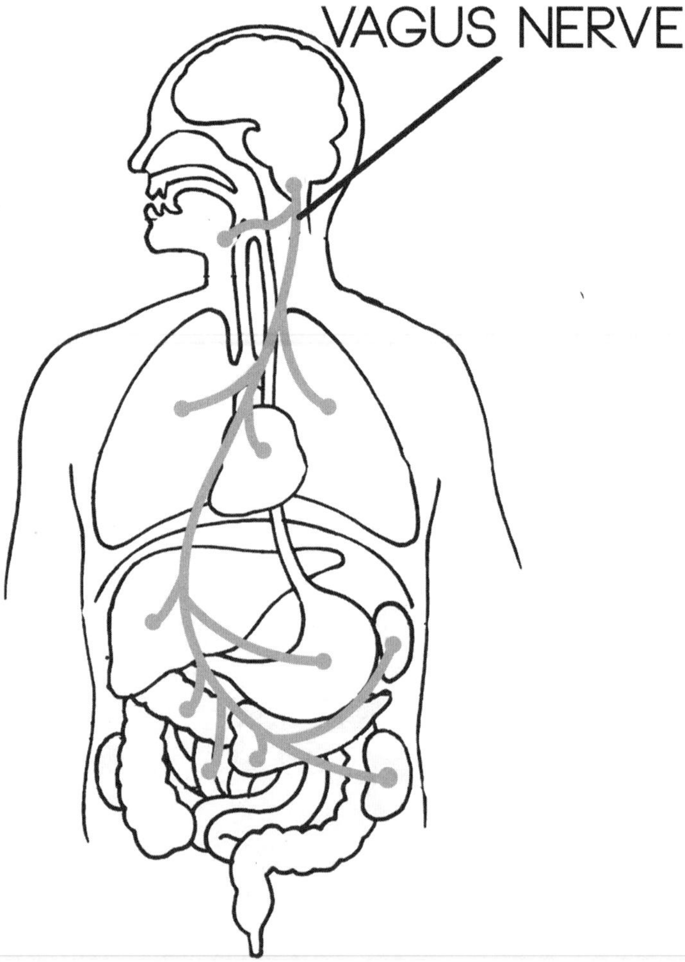

Figure 9 The Vagus Nerve

CHAPTER 8

Sleep Problems

Over the course of a lifetime, the pattern of sleep cycles changes. Young babies sleep up to 18 hours per day, and they spend much more time in deep, slow wave sleep. As children mature, they spend less time asleep and less time in deep slow wave sleep. Older adults may sleep only six to seven hours per night. What's more, adults often complain of early waking which they cannot avoid and spend very little time in slow wave sleep. In addition, stress and anxiety may cause sleeping problems or make existing problems worse.

Sleep Patterns and Age

Elderly people show an increase in disturbed sleep that can create a negative impact on their quality of life, mood, and alertness. Elderly people tend to be most vulnerable to sound disruptions during the night. As we get older the hypothalamus, which drives our circadian rhythm and regulates our body systems, gradually deteriorates. The melatonin levels drop also as a result. The electrical body can also deteriorate and sometimes a pacemaker can be used, which give small surges of an electrical current to help the heart to function. Most elderly people tend to experience physical disability, depression and respiratory problems.

Young children tend to adopt the circadian rhythm at about 3 months. This is when we notice they are getting into a sleeping routine. Sleep amounts decrease as the child gets older. Children are growing and developing rapidly at a young age. Sleep is crucial at this time therefore, and the growth hormone is released and active during sleep.

In women, the menstrual cycle may influence sleep-wake activity. Women's sleep cycles are greatly affected by pregnancy and other hormone effecting life stages like menopause.

How Sound Affects Sleep

Different types and levels of sounds can have either a positive effect or a negative effect on sleep. Noise from the environment like traffic, planes and trains can have an adverse effect on your sleep while gentle soothing music can diminish or drown out exterior noises. A partners snoring can create a lot of frustration and anxiety and result in sleep being lost.

The beginning stages of sleep prepare your body to shut down. During this stage, you can be easily awakened by noise. REM sleep on the other hand, is the deep stage of sleep where we dream. After the first 90 minutes of sleep we enter in REM for about 10 minutes. Each of your later REM sleep gets longer and more intense and deeper. When we are awoken during this stage, we often feel disoriented.

Men and women appear to have different sensitivities when it comes to being awakened by different noises. Men will wake up to alarming or threatening sounds like a street fight outside or a car alarm. Mothers are more likely to be aroused by their child's slightest whimper.

> ***This research shows that mothers respond more easily to the sound of their infant's restless movements during the night. It also shows that a mother's brain becomes more active when her name is sounded.***[73]

Children can arouse easily with new noises or loud sudden noises. Playing white noise is often a solution to drowning out noises and it also becomes a familiar noise. It can mask out these unwanted disturbing sounds.

Diabetes

Long term sleep deprivation can have serious impacts on your overall health. It can lead to obesity and Type 2 Diabetes. There are many studies to show that people who don't get enough sleep are prone to developing diabetes. People experiencing diabetes will usually have sleep problems. People with diabetes may also have Sleep Apneoa and maybe overweight.

When we are feeling stressed, overworked or don't get enough sleep, it increases our need for energy, and increases cortisol which sends out glucose into the bloodstream. When your blood sugar is high the kidneys try to get rid of it through urination. This will wake you during the night adding to the problem of fragmented sleep. Excessive urination will also lead you to feeling thirsty with a need to drink water during the night. High blood sugar increases your body temperature which is not ideal at night because the body temperature normally reduces for sleep.

Sugar spikes during the night lead to dips which activate cortisol. This balances the blood sugar with more glucose, and also stimulates the brain to wake up.

Reflux and Heartburn

When you overeat or eat heavy foods and then go to bed an hour or two later is a recipe for acid reflux. Heartburn is caused by acid reflux, which occurs when the ring of muscle that allows food into your stomach Lower Oesophageal Sphincter (LES) relaxes when it shouldn't. The result is acid from your stomach goes back up your oesophagus, which then causes the sensation of heartburn. Acid reflux can result in oesophageal cancer in the long term.[74]

Acid blockers may actually cause heartburn. This is because the stomach is not producing enough acid. The sphincter will only close or tighten when there is adequate levels of acid produced in the stomach.

Use a good quality Himalayan salt to help make enough hydrochloric acid in your stomach. Ensure that you are getting enough vitamin D, through sun exposure, foods or vitamins. This will help to support the immune system which helps with any Helicobacter pylori (H. pylori) infections in the stomach. Fermented foods and probiotics help with good bacteria, reducing inflammation and helping bowel flora helping to eliminate H. pylori bacteria.

Homemade Remedies

1. 1 teaspoon baking soda in a glass of water
2. Aloe Vera Juice
3. Slippery Elm – Sooths the gut and anti-inflammatory
4. Know your food triggers i.e. caffeine, alcohol, spicy foods. Eat more alkaline foods
5. 1 tablespoon of raw unfiltered apple cider vinegar in a glass of water[75]

Chronic heartburn is also known as Gastroesophageal Reflux Disease (GERD). For most people, heartburn is an occasional nuisance. But if you have heartburn regularly, it's likely a sign of GERD, a relentless condition in which stomach acids back up into the oesophagus.

The Dangerous affects of Night Time Heartburn

Heartburn at night can disrupt your sleep but it can also have some other consequential effects. Lying flat can aggravate the symptoms, and it can be painful. The epithelial cells in the oesophagus are a very thin layer, only one cell thick. The acid after travelling into the oesophagus can damage the lining, which may eventually lead to oesophageal cancer.

- Reduce stress. Stress can cause excess stomach acid
- Eat more alkaline foods like fruit and vegetables, cucumber. Avoid red meat.
- Avoid smoking. It causes the oesophageal sphincter to relax
- Some medications can increase stomach acid. Speak to your doctor

Fibromyalgia

Fibromyalgia causes pain throughout the whole body in the tissues, muscles and joints. Chronic Fatigue is often associated with Fibromyalgia. It is a very confusing and misunderstood condition and often goes unacknowledged and can be a very debilitating problem. It causes extreme daytime fatigue and the pain often interferes with sleep. 1 in 5 people with Fibromyalgia experience anxiety or depression which can further exasperate pain. Gentle exercise and massage treatments have been shown to help with the condition. Also, improving sleep usually reduces pain and fatigue and improves daytime functioning.

Pain

Many people who suffer with pain have great difficulty getting a restful sleep as a result of stress. Our muscles tighten when we experience stress and tension causing lactic acid which results in pain. Tension headaches along with neck and lower back pain are indicators of stress. Stress increases inflammation in the body and aggravates arthritis. Stress causes a cascade effect in the body when the brain signals the release of adrenaline and cortisol. These steroid hormones boost our blood sugar and oxygen levels, push more blood to the brain, and the result is increased alertness to pain signals. As a result of pain, people are getting shorter sleep durations adding to the already exasperating problem at hand. Those with acute or chronic pain are more likely to have sleep problems impact on their daily lives. Making sleep a priority, changing the sleeping environment and getting more sleep will help get a better quality of sleep even those who experience pain. Practice relaxation techniques and limit caffeine. See a doctor if pain is causing ongoing sleep disturbances.

High Blood Pressure

There are lots of things that can contribute to high blood pressure and lack of sleep is one of them. Sleeping reboots your whole system. It gives the nervous system a chance to rest and it helps to regulate hormones. We produce cortisol and adrenaline in response to stress which overtime can damage our blood vessels. We have seen that Sleep Apneoa causes a lack of oxygen in the blood which can lead to high blood pressure. Getting enough sleep helps to keep the body regulated and stable reducing the risk of high blood pressure.

Sleepwalking

Sleepwalking is very common in young children and often outgrown by their teenage years. This is because sleepwalking happens in deep sleep and children have longer deep sleep than adults. Sleepwalking is normally a result of lack of sleep, irregular sleep patterns, medication or sometimes emotional stress.

Grinding Teeth

Grinding teeth often happens at night and we are unaware it. If this is an ongoing occurrence then the teeth may be compromised or damaged. If the teeth are worn down from the constant grinding, it may result in getting canal treatment, implants or crowns. It can even cause Temporomandibular Joint (TMJ) problems resulting in your jaw coming out of alignment, difficulty chewing food, severe jaw pain, headaches and an array of other symptoms. You dentist can check for tell-tale signs and any damage done to the jaw, mouth or teeth.

Tips

- ***Avoid stimulant foods like caffeine and chocolate***
- ***Avoid alcohol***
- ***Avoid eating chewing gum***
- ***Relax your jaw at night by opening the mouth when you go to sleep***
- ***Try to be conscious of when you are tensing your jaw during the day***

It is common for children to grind their teeth when they are teething and when their adult teeth are coming in. This is temporary and usually passes. If you are concerned or your child complains of sensitivity or pain, bring them to the dentist for a check-up.

Tips for Children

- ***Try to de-stress your child, especially before going to bed.***
- ***Make sure they keep hydrated.***
- ***Try massaging the facial muscles especially under the ear where the jaw joint is.***

Bedwetting and Night Terrors

Night terror is when a child gets stuck between sleep cycles. It's a bolt of fear that occurs when transitioning from a deep NREM sleep into the next stage which is REM sleep. Nightmares occur in REM sleep and are quite different to night terrors, although they appear very similar. A child may recall a nightmare but can't remember a night terror. This is because there are no dreams or mental images during the deep NREM sleep stage. It is very difficult to wake a child up from the night terror as a result of the deep sleep and often the child will appear distressed, shouting, screaming or crying. Trying to wake them up will result in the child becoming disorientated and confused because they will have awoken from a deep sleep. In most cases, the child may need to go to the toilet but is unaware of this.

I personally experienced this quite a lot with my young child. As soon as she went to the toilet, still asleep, she went straight back to bed and slept soundly.

It is advised not to wake them up, but stay with them until it passes making sure they don't hurt themselves if they get into a rage. It is quite distressing for parents because they feel very helpless just waiting it out. If you feel it is happening regularly and you are worried, then seek help from your doctor.

Night terrors are caused by an over active nervous system. This happens when it is still developing. The night terrors normally dissipate as the child grows older.

Allergies

Allergic Rhinitis or Sinusitis occurs when airborne particles or allergens are breathed in and causes an irritation in the nasal mucous lining. This causes inflammation, irritation and congestion in the nose. Symptoms include sneezing, water and itchy eyes, congested or a runny nose.

There are many irritants that may cause nasal congestion or a stuffy nose. Irritants like cigarette smoke, air pollution, pollen and pet fur may trigger allergic reactions causing inflammation in the nasal membranes. The common cold may cause congestion which may lead to a bacterial or viral sinusitis infection. Mucus membranes that line the cavities in your nose produce a combination of mucus and fluid designed to wash away impurities. When the nose dries, it impedes this important function.

Here are some possible causes are nasal congestion:

- Sinusitis
- Dry air
- Cigarette Smoke
- Hormone Imbalance
- Household chemical cleaning products
- Personal care products
- Stress
- Colds and flu
- Allergies (food, Insect sting, drug allergy, atopic dermatitis)
- Allergic Rhinitis (Hayfever)
- Non-Allergic Rhinitis (Postnasal drip)

Sleep problems are common in people with Allergic Rhinitis. The severity of sleep deprivation depends on how sensitive you are to the allergies. Obstructive Sleep Apneoa (OSA), a sleep disorder in which breathing is briefly and repeatedly interrupted during sleep, is linked with Allergic Rhinitis. Nasal congestion contributes to the airways being too narrow making breathing more difficult and therefore difficulty sleeping. Sleep problems are linked to daytime fatigue, problems learning and memory, low mood, decreased productivity and a reduced overall quality of life.

Allergic Rhinitis (allergies) may occur year-round from household substances like dust mites or mould, or seasonally like in the case of hayfever. When it occurs seasonally it is usually caused by airborne pollen particles from trees, grass or weeds. The bacteria, Staphylococcus Aureus, can be found in the nasal passages of people with year-round Allergic Rhinitis, in which case can lead to further bacterial levels, increasing the allergy response.

Our microbiome (good bacteria) helps to modulate the immune responses when there is an infection or inflammation and is a very important part of our makeup. Over use of anti-biotics are killing our good bacteria and now becoming more resistant to bacterial infections.

Natural Remedy Solutions

Aromatherapy and essential oils can be used as a natural remedy to help fight against the symptoms of hayfever and allergies. Essential oils are known for their anti-inflammatory and decongestant properties to help fight against colds and flu. Using an oil diffuser or candle burner will act as a humidifier helping to keep the air moist and ridding the air of impurities. Essential oils help to tackle stress which is often a cause for the 'fight or flight' response, which leads to sugar imbalances in the blood and more inflammation in the body. Essential oils are not only known for their relaxing and uplifting properties they have natural antimicrobial properties as well.

A saline solution spray is often a good remedy helping to clean the nasal cavities, reduce the risk of infection and reduce excess mucus.

Plenty of rest and good quality sleep is vitally important to the body's innate healing abilities, fighting infections, reducing inflammation and balancing hormones.

Shift Work and Circadian Rhythm

Shift work and jet lag are two of the most commons ways to get your circadian rhythm out of sync.[76] If your circadian rhythm is broken, your vagus nerve will be broken to some degree. Light at night alters daily patterns of cortisol and the biological clock. Shift workers find it more difficult to sleep during the day because we are wired to sleep at night. Our circadian rhythm is at its lowest during the night making concentration more difficult and night work more challenging. Our circadian rhythm is at its strongest during the day making us more alert. However, with good sleep habits and a regular routine shift workers can get the sleep that they need.

Our external environment can help determine night and day. Our internal clocks also have their daily rhythms too. Jet lag is when the two don't match each other and the body gets confused. This is only a temporary problem because the body can adapt to the new surroundings and reset itself. Sunlight is the best way to get the body back on track. If you fly from west to east and your local arrival time is before 5am (local time), avoid the sun for a few hours. Your body will feel like it's midnight. Your body will mistake sunrise as sunset. Sunlight is the strongest factor to letting the body know when it is night and day.

CHAPTER 9

Sleeping with Diagnosed Diseases

People who think they sleep perfectly well and yet they are exhausted the next day may have some underlying health problems. Sleeping with diagnosed diseases can cause problems with sleeping, stress and interfering with the nightly brain function. It is important to know and understand how these diseases relate to you and what you can do to help alleviate them, reduce stress, reduce pain and get a better night sleep.

ADHD and Sleep

Attention Deficit Hyperactivity Disorder (ADHD) is hyperactivity in a child or adult making it difficult to focus and learn, control their behaviour, inattentive and compulsive. **There are approximately 60,000 children in Ireland living with ADHD according to 2010 figures from** IrishHealth.com.[77] There is an imbalance in the brain around the attention and activity area. This is what contributes to impulsiveness in children and it often gets them into trouble because they do things without thinking. Hyperactivity seems to lessen as they get older but the lack of attention and focus remain. Children often get very emotional about this behaviour because they can't control it and they feel they can't do things right like other children.

Children with ADHD are on the rise. Parents report that they are two to three times more likely to have problems with sleep, than children who do not have ADHD. Parents notice that when their child doesn't get enough sleep their behaviours are affected more the following day. In general, **children who have difficulties sleeping or who don't get enough sleep will have symptoms like that of ADHD and are often misdiagnosed with this condition, so be mindful of that.** Scientists are working on what is happening in the brain at night and how it affects sleep. Sleep is extremely important especially for children because they are still developing. **The growth hormone is released at night in the deep phases of sleep so this is vital for your child while they are growing and developing.** Sleep is as important as nutrition and exercise. It affects their behaviour quite dramatically since some children find it difficult to articulate a problem and it is even more difficult with lack of sleep. This can result in behavioural problems as the child gets frustrated. Other sleep problems reportedly associated with ADHD in children and adults include: - trouble falling asleep, trouble staying asleep, waking up in the middle of the night, sleepwalking, snoring, breathing difficulties, restless sleep, nightmares, daytime sleepiness and anxiety.

Often at night it is extremely difficult for children to settle down into a wind down routine before bed. This is a very important process when getting ready for bed. For children experiencing this condition, it is important to have a bedtime routine. This way they become familiar and automatically expect the routine.

When neurotransmitters are not healthy this will have an impact on ADHD. Low dopamine partially contributes to ADHD. Sleep is so extremely important for clearing out the brain at night. It takes out all the toxins and effectively cleans it up. The brain has its own system called the glymphatic system. *(See Chapter 3 – The Science of Sleep – section on The Brain and Sleep)*.

Get rid of electronics in the evening and at night. They should not be anywhere near a bedroom. Make the associating of a bedroom as a sleep haven, free of anything electrical, including radio alarm clocks and blinking lights. Do not charge anything in the bedroom and unplug electronics from the socket. When something is plugged in and the item is switched off, it still emits radiation into the room. This will interfere with your child's electrical field. *(See Chapter 6 – Sleep and Hormones – section on The Electrical Body).*

The brain waves need to slow down in preparation for sleep. When asleep the brain waves slow down even further for deep sleep and increase in amplitude. This is because the brain is so active at night sending signals to the body for all the healing, repairing and growing. It is important our electrical field is not impeded which will affect this important brain functioning in the body at night.

Neuroplasticity is the ability of the brain to form new neural pathways from learning or experiences. The lack of neuroplasticity could be a huge contributor to keeping us stuck in old patterns and in conditions like ADHD. Eat the right brain foods like omega 3's, essential minerals like magnesium, turmeric is a great anti-inflammatory and good for brain health and polyphenols (anti-oxidants) found in berries. Exercise is always good for the brain and re-wiring you brain with cognitive behavioural therapy. This will help you to focus on what makes you happy and change the way you think about things in a positive way. Body mind connection exercises are also effective like Tai Chi and yoga.

It is especially important to manage blood glucose levels during the day to stop elevated cortisol during the night. Cortisol will produce more glucose in the blood and cortisol is one of the 'fight or flight' steroid hormones waking us up. This causes stress and ongoing this can damage blood vessels. Eating healthy foods like omega 3's for brain health, complex carbohydrates, fresh fruit and vegetables. Avoid stimulants, fizzy drinks etc and eat protein early in the day to stabilise blood sugar levels during the day.

Essential oils to help children sleep are Roman Chamomile and Lavender. They are known for their soothing and relaxing properties. Put a few drops on some magnesium flakes and drop into a warm bath right before bed. You can also diffuse in the bedroom right throughout the night.

I like to put a couple of drops onto my daughter's soft toys when she is going asleep.

Children with this condition may be open to other sleep problems like snoring and sleepwalking or breathing difficulties. If you are concerned, visit your doctor.

Asthma and Sleep

Shortness of breath, wheezing and coughing make it very difficult to sleep at night. **According to Asthma Society of Ireland, 7.1% of the 18+ population have asthma and 18.9% of 13 – 15 year olds have asthma. Ireland has the fourth highest rates of asthma in the world.** Nocturnal asthma can be serious and will need a proper diagnoses and treatment from your doctor. Breathing can be worse when lying down. Air conditioning in a room at night can also trigger an attack so be mindful of that also.

There is also an increased risk of exposure to allergens, dust mites etc that can irritate the nasal passageways. This causes a sinusitis attack and can also trigger an asthma attack. Dust can contain mould, fibres, pet fur and dust mites. Carpets are notorious for dust mites. Get rid of them if possible and use wooden floors instead. Vacuum regularly and wash surfaces with a damp cloth. Use protective covers on your mattress and pillows. An essential oil diffuser can kill airborne germs and also keep dust mites at bay. Lavender is a gentle and safe oil to use for asthma. Use a little to start to make sure you are not overly sensitive to it. Dust mites love warm humid rooms so air the room out every day by opening the window. Pull back your bed covers after you get out of bed when it is still warm. You can make your bed when the warmth has gone. Wash the curtains regularly also.

Dementia and Sleep

There are many brain and neurological disorders that can contribute to sleeping difficulties. **There are 55,000 people in Ireland living with dementia according to the HSE from 2016 figures.**[78] There are 44 million people worldwide who experience dementia. Dementia is a term used to describe the overall degenerative diseases of the brain which results from brain cells dying and the connections between them dying off as well as plaque deposits on the brain causing complications. This stops the cells from communicating with each other so thinking, feelings, sleeping and behaviours are all affected.

Dementia symptoms can vary but can be a mixture of significantly impaired symptoms like loss of memory, the inability to focus, language difficulties, reasoning, visual perception and a great deal of stress as a result. The risk for developing dementia increases with age. 5% of 65 year olds may have dementia while a 90 year old may have a risk increase of 50%.[79] People with dementia usually live with family or a carer. They too will have a great deal of stress in their lives also.

Keeping your mind active as you get older will help to protect you against the disease. Eating the right healthy fats, like omega 3 (high in salmon) will help to reduce damage to the myelin sheets on the neurons, part of the nervous system, and help brain function. The circulatory system is vitally important for brain health because the blood vessels bring nutrients and oxygen to the brain. Damage to your blood vessels anywhere in your body has a profound affect on your brain. Protect your heart, blood pressure and blood sugar balance by eating healthily and getting enough sleep.

Sleep is the biggest and most effective ways of detoxifying the brain. In fact, it is the only way to detoxify the brain. This is done in the deep stages of sleep when we are in an unconscious state. This is the only time the brain's tissues can shrink enough to allow the Cerebral Spinal Fluid (CSF) to circulate around the brain and remove all the toxins.

Types of dementia diseases are Motor Neuron Disease, Parkinson's Disease, Stroke and Epilepsy. Motor Neuron Disease is a degeneration of motor neurons involving the voluntary muscles causing a weakness in muscle movement. Parkinson's Disease on the other hand, affects the nervous system and usually starts with shaking or tremor in the hand. It disrupts the signals to voluntary muscles.

Sleeping at night is a very active process even though we appearing to be totally at rest. The hypothalamus and brain are very active and neurons are busy sending signals back and forth throughout the night. In fact the brain is busier at night time than during the day. Sleep movement, breathing, parasomnias (sleep walking and nightmares) are all problems encountered by those with neurological disorders. Parasomnias may also trigger other sleep disorders like Sleep Apneoa. If you notice your loved one forgetting a lot, don't ignore it and see a doctor. The earlier you get treatment the better to possibly help prevent it progressing too fast or temporarily alleviating symptoms.

Alzheimers and Sleep

Alzheimer's disease is a form of dementia that affects the brain. **There are 55,000 people in Ireland living with dementia of which two thirds have Alzheimer's**. It affects 1 in 10 people over the age of 65. The brain region called the Hippocampus is the centre of learning and memory in the brain, and the brain cells in this region are often the first to be damaged. That's why memory loss is often one of the earliest symptoms of Alzheimer's.

Alzheimer's is known primarily for the person losing their memory. This is the first affect Alzheimer's has on a person. It is a progressive disease which kills off the brain cells and eventually affects other areas of the brain affecting language, problem solving and moods. It begins in the hippocampus where plaques and tangles are accumulated. Your brain is very much affected by how much quality of sleep you are getting. We know sleep is important for the detoxification of the brain. We know that the lymphatic system clears toxins in the body but the brain relies on the CSF. This is part of thc brain's glymphatic system which clears out any of the bad guys. In particular, it clears out the toxic beta amyloid protein which is known to build up in people with Alzheimer's. *(See Chapter 3 – The Science of Sleep – section on The Brain and Sleep).*

We know neuroplasticity is the ability of the brain to form new neural pathways from learning or experiences. This is also an important process for the elderly to help them retain long term memories also known as memory consolidation. In this way, it is important to form different neural pathways to help remember something or someone. Do regular brain training exercises. By simply staying engaged in new activities, learning new skills and meeting new people will help the brain stay focused and make new neural pathways. The key to neuroplasticity is to learn new things every day. This changes the structure of the brain. The more neural pathways you form the less chance you have of forgetting.

Exercise is very important for the brain to keep the circulation flowing and to get oxygen to the brain. Also, good brain foods like omega 3's, anti-oxidants, turmeric and magnesium.

Epilepsy and Sleep

Epilepsy is a neurological disorder involving an electrical interference which results in an episode of convulsion triggered by a sensory disturbance. **It is estimated that there are over 37,000 people in Ireland with epilepsy and 50 million worldwide according to Epilepsy Ireland.**[80] Seizures are very sensitive to sleep patterns, the hormonal and the electrical activity changes that happen during the night. The brain waves slow down entering into the different brain wave states. (See Chapter 3 – The Science of Sleep – section on Brain Waves and Sleep Cycles). The brain is actually more active during the night than during the day. About 1 in 4 people who have epilepsy have seizures during the night which effects the sleep cycles, resulting in loss of deep sleep and contributing more to the epilepsy condition.

Not getting enough sleep can trigger seizures which will make you more likely to have a seizure. People who often have their first attack as a result of staying up all night studying for an exam and having an attack during the day.[81] Find out how much sleep you need. In general for an adult it is between 7 – 9 hours. If you get good quality sleep, you should feel rested when you wake up.

- Get some exercise early in the day to help the circulation and oxygen flow to the brain.
- Adapt good sleeping habits, do a gentle wind down routine every night.
- Eat the right foods for brain health, cut out stimulants like sugar and caffeine.

Always see your doctor if you experience attacks or are concerned.

Conclusion

There are many diagnosed diseases and disorders that affect the ability to sleep well on a regular basis. Most of the time stress, a busy lifestyle and the environment have a big impact on the ability to sleep well even with diagnosed conditions. Adapting lifestyle and environmental changes and how we feel about sleep all contribute to getting a good night's sleep.

CHAPTER 10

ENVIRONMENTAL INFLUENCES

Our internal and external environment can determine how well your circadian rhythm is in sync and this includes noise, food, sleep, temperature and lighting. Your body's sleep-wake cycle, or circadian rhythm, plays a vital role in many body processes. This affects our mood, mental alertness, our energy and also our weight. Just like we have our sleep cycles at night, we also have our cycles during our wakefulness.

Light and Circadian Rhythm

Our body is interconnected with the earth. In Traditional Chinese Medicine (TCM), the Chinese clock and circadian rhythms are a daily cycle of biological activity and behavioural changes that follow 24-hour cycle, responding primarily to light and darkness and so we are related to our environment in deep ways. These rhythms are often out of sync as a result of the influence of our environment. These disruptions or imbalances affect our sleep/wake cycle, endocrine function, and other body functions.

When the light bulb was invented by Thomas Edison in the late 19th century, we started to stay up later. This started to affect our sleep patterns. The most important time for deep rest is 10pm - 3am. This is when the gallbladder and liver are regenerating and the liver filters out toxins. It releases and transforms the stress hormones, adrenaline, cortisol and insulin. It is so important for these stress hormones to be filtered and broken down.

Problems getting to sleep at night often arise from worrying, sorrow and the heart wandering. In other words, something is worrying you and there is something you need to release. Sometimes people experience falling asleep as a simple process but find they wake up wide awake in the middle of the night. Is it an aspect of life that wakes you up? Sometimes we get caught up in a mental loop about a loss, lack of happiness, a job, or a relationship. We often don't even realise our own feelings. And sometimes we just need to listen to what our bodies are trying to tell us or to be conscious of the emotion we are experiencing.

If you are a sensitive person, you can also feel someone else's pain, hurt or anger. Don't attach yourself to the person by trying to 'fix' their problem. In doing that, their feelings become yours. You are taking on that energy. It is important to recognise this. Ask yourself, "Is this my stuff or does it belong to someone else?" When we know it doesn't belong to us, we don't make it personal and it is easier to let go of the feeling and it doesn't get stuck in our energy.

Each meridian is linked to particular parts of the body, mechanisms of the body, thoughts and emotions. There are key responsibilities (aspects of life) connected to each meridian. Consider the emotions related to each meridian and see if you can find any relationships. Each organ in Chinese medicine has an emotional component and a spiritual component.

- Liver rules the emotion of anger
- Kidney rules the emotion of fear
- Heart rules the emotion of joy.

When a person is having a difficult time in their life physically, there may be an emotional aspect to it. Your emotions and your spirit are connected, you can't separate it. Always be curious about your body and how it works and what messages it is trying to give you. Don't give up on it, co-operate with it. When your body is irritating you, it is usually trying to tell you something.

Sleep-wake Homeostasis

Body temperature is determined by circadian rhythm. It naturally falls at night time allowing the body to prepare for sleep. The body will begin to gradually increase the body temperature a few hours before it is time for the body to wake up, helping to stimulate the body to wake. This process works along with the circadian rhythm and light.

Yin and Yang

Understanding the key aspects of Chinese medical theory is critical to appreciate why we use it. There are 6 main areas in Chinese medicine. Yin and Yang, the 5 elements, the 12 meridians, the organs which relate to the meridians, the acupoints which are the access points on the meridians and 'qi', which is the energy we are interested in when we are working from the Chinese point of view.

Yang	Yin
Fire	Water
Sun	Moon
Black	White
Light	Darkness
Day	Night
Red	Blue
Hot	Cool
Loud	Quiet
Angry	Timid

Table 4 Yin and Yang

The most fundamental area and most effective area which everything comes back to are Yin and Yang. They are fundamental forces of the universes and everything comes back to Yin and Yang. Polarities are two opposite forces, dualistic; in order to understand daytime, you have to understand night-time. The two are dependent on each other. The solution to feeling 'wired and tired' (too much Yang) is to balance Yin and Yang.

We can use two acupoints to balance Yin and Yang. Heart 7 and Kidney 3 are probably the most effective. Heart 7 is on the heart meridian and related to the heart organ. The heart organ is related to fire one of the 5 elements and the month of summer. Chinese medicine teaches us to live in harmony with the seasons. Each month has its own characteristics and summer is the most active of all the seasons with long days and lots of sunshine. Summer is about growth and expansion. Kidney 3 is on the kidney meridian and related to the kidney organs. Winter represents the most Yin aspect in Chinese medicine. Yin is cold, dark and slow, with inward energy. Winter is associated with the kidneys which hold our body's vital energy. Kidney is related to water one of the 5 elements. Water is cooling and flowing.

Holding these two points with intention and being present, breathing in and out slowly, will balance the flow of energy (qi) helping to create a harmony between Yin and Yang and therefore help with sleeping. *See Figure 10 Heart 7, Figure 11 Kidney 3.*

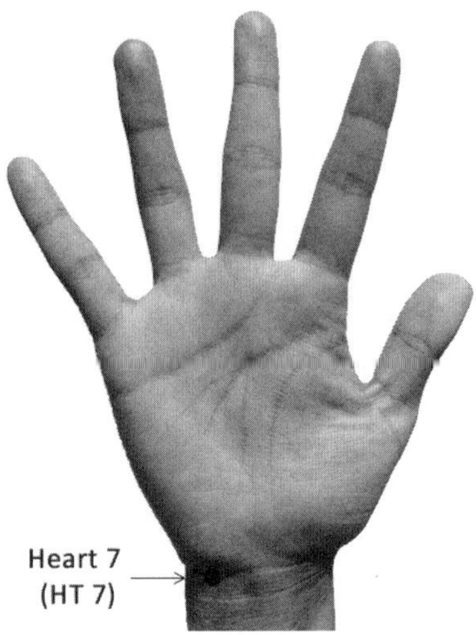

Figure 10 Heart 7

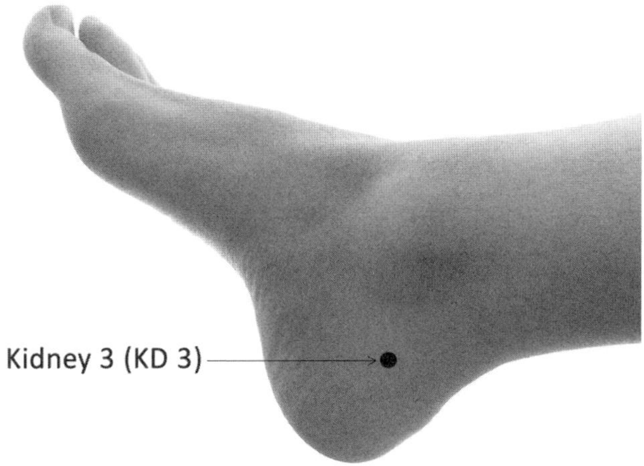

Figure 11 Kidney 3

Jet Lag and Shift Work

There are several different reasons why people are not getting good quality sleep. Sleeping better affects every organ system and disease state. Jet lag and shift work affect our circadian cycle and therefore your sleep. Our body is hard wired for night and day so it has to work hard to adjust to these types of environments you are subjected to. Each organ system is active for a two hour period in the biological body clock cycle in two twelve hour cycles during day and night. For example, the liver is most active at night when the body is resting between 1am and 3am. If you are working at night, the detoxification process does not work optimally. Sleep is vital at this time for physical and emotional detoxification. In addition, the immune system is suppressed with the less good quality sleep. Disease cells and cancer cells may grow quicker with ongoing sleep deprivation.

Individuals are trying to sleep when their internal clock is trying to stay awake. This will cause excessive sleepiness and bring on micro sleeps which can be very dangerous to the individual and our society. People working in this category are pilots, air traffic controllers, doctors, police and public safety workers.

Sleep Disorders and Diseases

There are many physical and mental health disorders and diseases that contribute to difficulties sleeping or getting good quality sleep. Our body is in a completely different state at night time compared to during the day. We are more electrically active with brain signals while the body is relaxing and healing.

Stress and anxiety are often related to sleep disorders and diseases and can often lead to depression. When we are constantly in this state, our brain is programmed to always respond to anything that is threatening us and so we tend to only sleep very lightly. We miss out on our much needed healing and restorative deep sleep.

Substances

There are other substances that keep up awake or prevent us from having a good quality night's sleep. Caffeine found in stimulant drinks, coffee and tea is a common culprit. Smoking can stimulate the nervous system and prevent you from winding down. People say they need it to relax. When you haven't smoked for a period of time, it creates a withdrawal response from the nicotine which makes you feel like you need one to relax. Alcohol is another substance *(See Chapter 2 - When I Just Can't Sleep - section on Drinking)*.

Medications can interfere with sleep and our sleep drive, because they always have side effects. They are usually blocking some other process in the body. Anti-histamine medication is another one because histamine is our wake up neurotransmitter. If we are experiencing allergies during the day and take anti-histamine medications, we block the histamines and this causes drowsiness.

Your Bedroom Environment

Make your bedroom conducive to sleep. The bedroom is a place of serenity and peace. It is our haven of privacy, our space and it's where we go to get total relaxation and rest. Using the five senses, here are the top five senses tips:

1. Sound - Use White Noise

White noise is a combination of frequencies you can hear with the human ear. It has some similarities to rain, water and the wind. Babies and children find white noise very soothing. This is because the noise inside the womb is very similar. It is usually used to mask out unwanted noises. White noise contains all the audible frequencies so it keeps the ears busy with all the different sounds and therefore not able to be aware of any other unwanted outside sounds that would normally wake you up. You can also listen to white noise from nature like waterfalls, rain and oceans.

If snoring is a factor, decongesting can help. Take a steam inhalation before bed to help open up the airways. Use a saline nasal spray and a humidifier with essential oils. Lying on the side can help open up the airways, losing body weight.

2. Touch/Feel - Room Temperature

Our body temperature lowers at night to help us prepare for sleep. The ideal room temperature is between 17°C and 19°C. Ensure you have a comfortable and supportive mattress and pillows. This will help support the neck and spine. If you feel stiff when you get out of bed, then you need a new mattress. Invest in new sheets and pillow cases and even new nightwear.

3. Sight/Light – Blue light

The blue light from our computer screens or mobile devices stops the production of melatonin, our sleep hormone. Install an app called 'Flux', which will take out the blue light according to the daylight hour.

4. Smell/Aroma

Aromatherapy essential oils can help to promote sleep.

Best Essential Oils for Sleep

- **Lavender** has been used for thousands of years. It contains over 200 chemical constituents and so offers something for almost every symptom while balancing the root cause. Lavender is known for its very relaxing and calming properties.
- **Roman Chamomille** helps the brain to relax but also helps the digestive system to relax. Great for muscle cramps and a great anti-inflammatory.
- **Vetiver** works directly on the nervous system. Also good for neurological problems like ADHD, dementia, autism. Great for anger and hysteria.
- **Ylang Ylang** is a natural aphrodisiac, helping to improve your mood. Great for helping to release locked up emotions. Just what you need before going to bed.
- **Cedarwood** helps to release emotions being processed by the liver at night

5. Taste

Spicy food can lead to Indigestion which can translate by the brain into a nightmare.

Electro Magnetic Frequencies (EMF)

We all know that sleep is so important for our health and happiness and one of the factors affecting good quality sleep is the electromagnetic field in your bedroom. Our immune system is very busy at night doing all its repair work. Keeping our cells healthy is extremely important because without this work, they would be damaged, die off or mutate. If this happened we would be subjected to diseases and infections. Our brains are very busy at night sending all the signals to the body with instructions. We are electrical beings and so EMF's in the bedroom can interfere dramatically with these processes.

Mobile Phones

Our mobile phone is constantly sending out signals and receiving signals for Wi-Fi and data and of course our phone calls.

> ***At a recent event I organised, 90% of the audience said they bring their mobile phones to bed.***

Most of who use it as an alarm clock. Turn your phone off or onto flight mode if you need to use it for an alarm clock.

Cordless Phones

Cordless phones act like a mini cell phone tower. You do not want this near your head when you are sleeping at night.

Lighting

Compact Fluorescent Light-Bulbs (CFL) emits electromagnetic radiation as a by-product of the energy saving mechanism. If you put an AM radio next to the light bulb you will hear the interference in the form of radiation. Use incandescent bulbs instead of using CFLs.

Electrical Devices

Unplug any electrical devices in your bedroom. Even an electric blanket can emit radiation. Do not charge anything in your room even if it is switched off. The AC adapter, used for charging devices, can emit very strong electrical fields.

Wi-Fi and Electromagnetic Radiation

Turn off Wi-Fi in the home at night. A wireless router used for your internet access, transmits a radio frequency signal. There are over 10,000 mobile phone antennae in Ireland, transmitting microwave radiation constantly.[82] There are many masts and antennae scattered around Ireland and some not so obvious. If you live near one of these, you can invest in special shielding that may help to at least reduce it. All this negative energy from the environment is also called 'orgone energy'.[83] Orgonite is a substance that comes in all shapes and sizes and ultimately it changes this negative energy into positive energy. This negative energy comes from masts and towers, Wi-Fi routers and even geopathic stress areas. Orgonite is typically made of metals and crystals (organic and inorganic materials).

Geopathic Stress

Geopathic stress has a major effect on our bodies especially at night when we are in the same location all night. It blocks our neurotransmitters in particular, serotonin. It also impedes our immune system. The first and often the most common indicator of geopathic stress is if it is taking longer than normal to overcome a cold, or a simple procedure. Orgonite can help but it would be much better to move the bed in a different location. Get someone into your house if you suspect geopathic stress, (and it is quite common) who can help detect it and advise you.

All of these different environmental factors affect how we sleep, either the amount of times we wake up or the length of sleep we get, and how deep our sleep is.

Sleeping Tools

Use sleep tracking apps like 'Sleep Time' to help track sleep patterns and identify some sleeping habits. It can measure your own sleeping phases and how your body movements are during the night. This app also lets you set a time to wake up and 'Sleep Time' will wake you up during your lightest sleeping phase so you will not feel disoriented and instead feeling more refreshed.

Improve Sleep Quality

Sleep is a very important part of your daily routine. After all, we sleep for one third of our lives. Sleep is as essential for life as food, air and water. However, sleep helps to connect the physical essentials to our spiritual necessities helping us to have happiness in our lives and love life.

Keep a sleep journal to help identify which area of sleep you are having a problem with or use a sleep app like 'Sleep Time'. It could be getting asleep or waking up too much during the night or maybe you wake up very early in the morning and can't go back asleep. By keeping a journal and recording these events over a two week period will help identify which areas to work on.

We need to think about the different stages of sleep for quality sleep. One cycle takes approximately 90 minutes. We need between 3 – 5 full sleep cycles for good quality sleep. Each sleep stage has its own specific brain waves and neurological activity. Stage 2 is repeated in all cycles and we spend most of our time in this stage in total during the night. Stage 2 helps keep the cycle together. Stages 3 and 4 are the deep slow wave sleep where all the healing and repair is done and this occurs mostly during the first half of the night. REM sleep deepens and becomes longer during the later stages of the night.

7 Step Summary of Sleeping Tips

Step 1. Stick to a Routine

Adapt a sleeping ritual (see below) at least an hour before you go to bed. Go to bed at the same time and wake up at the same time, including weekends. By doing this, your body will automatically know when it is time to go to sleep and wake up. You can even wake up automatically without and alarm clock.

Step 2. Caffeine

Stop drinking coffee by 2pm. It has a half-life of 8 - 10 hours. This means it is very slow to metabolise in your system and will affect your sleep. Some people are more sensitive than others. Caffeine is also in many energy drinks and stimulating foods like dark chocolate. Caffeine prevents you from falling asleep but if it is still in the system, it will prevent you from getting good quality sleep.

Step 3. Avoid Alcohol

Alcohol makes you feel sleepy but prevents you from deep sleep. Alcohol is a diuretic making you dehydrated and probably waking you to go to the bathroom.

Step 4. Exercise/Movement

Don't exercise too late for the purpose of making you tired. This is a big mistake because you will have a lot of adrenaline in your system. Most professional athletes have this problem because they exercise for long hours. Instead, exercise earlier in the day. This will help you make feel good endorphins including serotonin, required to make your sleep hormone melatonin. Do some relaxation exercises before going to bed whatever that is for you.

Step 5. Sunlight

We get energy from the sun as well as food. Get outdoors if you are feeling very fatigued. This will help your wake/ sleep drive. Getting outdoors will also give you much needed oxygen for your cellular activity.

Step 6. Diet

Eat wisely. Eat protein early in the day to get the amino acids needed for brain function and neurotransmitter activities. Eat complex carbohydrates in the later afternoon or evening to give your thyroid and adrenals some energy. Eat healthy fats, anti-oxidants, cut out sugar and refined foods as much as possible. Ensure you get good quality Probiotics into your diet.

I personally love kefir in smoothies, or with a fruit salad.

The microbiome is the most metabolically active organ (some people like to call it an organ because there is a huge population of them) in your body at night. It enables good gut brain connection and the gut is home to where most of our neurotransmitters are made. It also helps vagus nerve stimulation helping to relax us. Fasting is also a great way to stimulate the vagus nerve and help give the digestive system a rest. Drink room temperature water to hydrate the brain. This also helps to stop the morning fog. Do not eat late at night.

Step 7. Your Bedroom

Make your bedroom a sleeping haven. Make sure your room is not cluttered. Clean it regularly to get rid of dust mites and other possible allergens. Change your sheets regularly. Turn off any electrical device, reduce any possibilities of Electromagnetic Radiation (EMF), and make your room dark and cool.

Sleeping Ritual

Preparing for sleep is a highly effective and natural way of winding down, helping to promote a state of relaxation and calm. It involves winding down, setting the environment, grounding and shutting off electrical devices.

Relaxation Exercises

Prepare for bedtime with relaxing techniques. Doing this every night, even for just a few minutes, will help to establish a routine and these techniques will become habitual. Here are some relaxing exercises you can do:

- **Breathing** – Breathing connects our mind and body through the vagus nerve. By stimulating the vagus nerve you can reduce stress and anxiety and therefore reduce cortisol production and inflammation in the body. This deep breathing, also called 'slow abdominal breathing', is something that you can do at anytime, anywhere. It is especially good to do before you go to bed as part of your wind down. *(See Chapter 8 – Sleep Problems – section on The Vagus Nerve)*.
- **Meditation and Grounding** – Meditation can be done in various ways from a slow gentle walking meditation to sitting in the lotus position listening to a guided meditation. It's different for everyone but it is all about becoming aware of your internal messages and gut instincts. We must slow down and be still, away from the hectic lifestyle because it is only then that we can listen. Notice where you are and

bring your attention to your body. Focus on your breathing. By doing this you are grounding and plugging back into yourself and the earth. The one thing we are eliminating when we meditate is stress. Stress inhibits melatonin, our sleep hormone.

- **Visualising** – Visualising can't be underestimated. The power of visualising tricks the brain into thinking everything is aright. Our brain is hard wired to protect us and so that is why we live in fear a lot of the time.
    - We are afraid to do something new or change a current situation.
    - We like to have control and this is true when we are going asleep.
    - We have thoughts that we must go to sleep by a certain time or else something will happen.
    - We will be tired the next day or won't be able to get up on time or we will look wrecked.

The list goes on. Instead use the power of choice and visualise. Choose to let it happen and accept things the way they are when you are in bed. Sounds easy, I know, but trust me.

I have done this and it works.

Let those annoying thoughts roll around your head, allow them to be there. Then there will be no resistance and it will dissipate. **Just image, going to bed with no worries. How would it feel? You CAN do it.**

- **Hot Bath** – We hear a lot about the importance of calcium but magnesium is equally just as important, especially when it comes to sleep. We are 85% deficient in magnesium so it is always a good idea to consider magnesium in your diet or a magnesium bath before you go to bed. It's also known as 'nature's tranquilliser' and helps with symptoms such as anxiety, irritability and other mood changes. Good food sources of magnesium include whole grains, dark green vegetables and nuts. Magnesium helps to relax the nervous system and all the tension in your body. It's also good for restless legs. Use in addition with relaxing essential oils for its wonderful aromas and relaxing properties. Your body normally drops in temperature in preparation for sleep. When you get out of your body, the drop in temperature educes this process, helping you to get asleep.

Conclusion

We have seen the importance of sleep and all the affects it has on the body. Our brain is more active during the night than it is during the day sending lots of instructions around the body for healing, growing and repairing. It is an extremely active process. It is like rebooting a computer, wiping us clean and starting from fresh.

We have seen how sleeping disorders and diseases can interfere with good quality sleep, however in a lot of cases this can be minimised or possibly even eliminated. We looked at how the foods we eat have an enormous impact of our health overall and how we sleep. Putting all this information together helps us better understand how sleep works and therefore manipulate our situation to make it work for us.

Our sleep is a natural process and many of us still try to control it instead of just letting it happen naturally. It's the very struggle that is stopping us from getting asleep. Our feelings and emotions get in the way of this and contribute to putting up the road blocks.

We must start noticing things around us, being mindful and conscious of how we are living. Only then when we notice, we are aware of what's going on and how we are being. When we accept things for the way they are, the struggle lessens. We don't try to control situations so much and let things be.

Many diseases today come from deep suppressed emotions. We live in a very bitter and angry society that many will drink alcohol to forget these emotions or smoke cigarettes to numb the nervous system. Many of us wake between 1am and 3am in the morning which is when the liver is most active detoxifying our emotions among other toxic chemicals in our body. Women and men have different responses or reactions to emotions. Women never stop talking about who did what to who, they are sometimes referred to as drama queens and love to be heard. Men on the other hand are quite the opposite. They suppress their emotions more and so they are not expressed. They tend to get fierce angry when they experience an angry episode after suppressing for so long. We all have feminine and masculine energies that we must balance in our energy. Feminine is that nurturing, creative, quiet reflective energy and the masculine is that get up and go, action energy and strength. We all need a bit of both.

You have the choice to change your perception on sleep and apply what you have learned. This is a matter for physically making simples changes, getting into a routine and also to think positively and see a positive outcome. We can read and learn all we want, however, at the end of the day you must do it. So take control and do something however small today to get on the path of wellness and a better more productive night's sleep. You will be glad you did and so will your family and friends because you will be a much happier and healthier person. You will have your life back with the ability to do anything you want!

Wishing you peaceful dreams!

End Notes and Resources

1 http://uk.businessinsider.com/thomas-edison-winston-churchill-sleeping-habits-2015-2

2 http://www.rsa.ie/en/RSA/Road-Safety/Campaigns/Current-road-safety-campaigns/Drunk-With-Tiredness/

3 http://www.rsa.ie/en/RSA/Road-Safety/Campaigns/Archived-Campaigns/Drink-Driving/Drink-Driving---Fast-Facts/

4 http://www.rsa.ie/en/RSA/Road-Safety/Campaigns/Archived-Campaigns/Drink-Driving/Drunk-Driving-Myths--Facts/

5 https://www.ncbi.nlm.nih.gov/pubmed/2928622

6 https://www.mind-body-health.net/burnout.shtml

7 https://www.ncbi.nlm.nih.gov/pmc/articles/PMC3756673/

8 Alcohol Clin Exp Res. 2013 Apr;37(4):539-49.

9 https://sleepfoundation.org/sleep-topics/how-alcohol-affects-sleep

10 http://www.livestrong.com/article/408524-are-energy-drinks-bad-for-your-liver/

11 http://www.thelist.com/42047/false-things-sleep-always-thought-true/s/a-bit-of-snooze-button-sleep-will-make-you-feel-better

12 https://www.urmc.rochester.edu/news/story/3956/to-sleep-perchance-to-clean.aspx

13 https://www.ncbi.nlm.nih.gov/pmc/articles/PMC2813509/

14 https://www.nih.gov/news-events/nih-research-matters/how-sleep-clears-brain

15 http://healthysleep.med.harvard.edu/healthy/science/how/neurophysiology

16 https://nootriment.com/acetylcholine/

17 http://healthysleep.med.harvard.edu/healthy/science/what/sleep-patterns-rem-nrem

18 http://www.wikihow.com/Lucid-Dream

19 http://www.isat.ie/

20 https://academic.oup.com/jcem/article-lookup/doi/10.1210/jcem.87.7.8663

21 https://www.ncbi.nlm.nih.gov/pmc/articles/PMC2635574/

22 https://www.sciencedaily.com/releases/2013/06/130603114144.htm

23 http://www.webmd.com/brain/restless-legs-syndrome/restless-legs-syndrome-rls#1

24 http://www.mayoclinic.org/tests-procedures/ferritin-test/details/why-its-done/icc-20271953

25 https://www.peoplespharmacy.com/2017/05/04/how-much-tonic-water-must-you-drink-to-ease-leg-cramps/

26 http://www.lincoln.ac.uk/news/2012/12/619.asp

27 https://www.helpguide.org/articles/sleep/sleeping-pills-and-natural-sleep-aids.htm

28 http://www.medbroadcast.com/channel/medications-and-your-health/what-drug-label-warnings-mean/may-cause-drowsiness

29 http://www.healthline.com/health/food-nutrition/valerian-root#safety7

30 https://www.ncbi.nlm.nih.gov/pubmed/10737183

31 https://www.ncbi.nlm.nih.gov/pubmed/9566605

32 http://www.mayoclinic.org/diseases-conditions/insomnia/in-depth/insomnia-treatment/art-20046677

33 http://articles.mercola.com/sites/articles/archive/2010/05/29/overthecounter-sleep-meds-are-not-effective.aspx

34 http://articles.mercola.com/sites/articles/archive/2013/10/31/sleep-brain-

detoxification.aspx

35 http://www.webmd.com/sleep-disorders/guide/understanding-the-side-effects-of-sleeping-pills#1

36 http://www.webmd.com/sleep-disorders/guide/understanding-the-side-effects-of-sleeping-pills#2

37 https://www.boundless.com/biology/textbooks/boundless-biology-textbook/the-endocrine-system-37/types-of-hormones-210/lipid-derived-amino-acid-derived-and-peptide-hormones-793-12028/

38 http://www.sciencedirect.com/topics/page/Thyroid-stimulating_hormone

39 https://www.youtube.com/watch?v=w1kIQ61zCtQ

40 http://www.mayoclinic.org/diseases-conditions/hyperthyroidism/basics/causes/con-20020986

41 http://www.mayoclinic.org/diseases-conditions/goiter/symptoms-causes/dxc-20264595

42 http://articles.mercola.com/sites/articles/archive/2017/06/17/our-daily-dose-fluoride-documentary.aspx

43 http://articles.mercola.com/sites/articles/archive/2012/02/01/is-this-one-of-natures-most-powerful-detoxification-tools.aspx

44 https://wellnessmama.com/14892/boost-thyroid-function/

45 https://chriskresser.com/the-gluten-thyroid-connection/

46 https://draxe.com/10-ways-balance-hormones-naturally/

47 http://www.greenmedinfo.com/blog/do-you-know-your-estrogen-eq

48 https://www.hormonesbalance.com/articles/hormones-cause-cancers-women/

49 http://raypeat.com/articles/articles/ru486.shtml

50 http://www.biospiritual-energy-healing.com/vibrational-frequency.html

51 https://youtu.be/U2VOLh1a-TI

52 http://circ.ahajournals.org/content/135/9/e96?dm_i=VOQ,4VWMG,J5EXAQ,IHYNU,1

53 http://www.webmd.com/vitamins-supplements/ingredientmono-936-dong%20quai.aspx?activeingredientid=936&

54 http://www.livestrong.com/article/355002-side-effects-of-aspartame-in-diet-soda/

55 http://sydney.edu.au/news-opinion/news/2016/07/13/why-artificial-sweeteners-can-increase-appetite.html

56 https://www.ncbi.nlm.nih.gov/pubmed/12662130

57 https://patient.info/health/generalised-anxiety-disorder-leaflet

58 http://www.webmd.com/anxiety-panic/guide/anxiety-disorders#1

59 https://www.verywell.com/what-is-a-neurotransmitter-2795394

60 https://www.aware.ie/information/resources/lectures/upcoming-aware-lectures/

61 https://www.ncbi.nlm.nih.gov/pubmed/14658968?dopt=AbstractPlus

62 http://www.sciencedirect.com/science/article/pii/S0301051101000904

63 http://www.bbc.com/news/health-37166293?SThisFB

64 http://www.jneurosci.org/content/33/17/7234

65 https://www.verywell.com/free-radicals-2507225

66 http://www.foodforthebrain.org/alzheimers-prevention/methylation-and-homocysteine.aspx

67 https://www.verywell.com/all-about-vitamin-k-benefits-and-uses-89528

68 https://www.verywell.com/the-benefits-of-vitamin-c-supplements-89083

69 http://divinehealthfromtheinsideout.com/2013/09/stress-and-mineral-depletion/

70 https://www.ncbi.nlm.nih.gov/pmc/articles/PMC3079864/

71 http://www.vivo.colostate.edu/hbooks/pathphys/endocrine/hypopit/lhfsh.html

72 http://www.prevention.com/health/health-concerns/how-fiber-feeds-your-gut-and-your-health

73 http://www.cell.com/neuron/fulltext/S0896-6273(00)00169-0

74 http://articles.mercola.com/sites/articles/archive/2014/11/15/dangers-late-night-eating.aspx

75 http://everydayroots.com/heartburn-remedies

76 https://selfhacked.com/2015/09/06/what-it-means-to-keep-to-a-circadian-rhythm/

77 http://www.irishhealth.com/article.html?id=17899

78 http://www.hse.ie/eng/services/list/4/olderpeople/dementia/about-dementia/dementia-stats/

79 http://dementia.ie/information/what-is-dementia

80 http://www.epilepsy.ie/

81 https://www.helpguide.org/harvard/medical-causes-of-sleep-problems.htm

82 https://iervn.com/mwrfradiation/masts-antennae/

83 https://www.orgoneenergy.org/blogs/news/the-purpose-of-an-orgone-generator-1